RED, WHITE, BLUE, AND CATHOLIC

STEPHEN P. WHITE

Cheers for *Red, White, Blue, and Catholic*

"We need to be salt and light and leaven, even in politics, in and out of election season. Stephen White offers an accessible and yet urgent guide to doing the crucial work of Christian citizenship with love."

— **Kathryn Jean Lopez,** senior fellow,
National Review Institute

"Drawing on Catholic social teaching, White—writing with admirable clarity and in engaging prose—reminds us that Catholic citizenship is to be lived out locally and nationally every day, as well as on voting day."

— **Carson Holloway,** political scientist, author,
and contributor to *ThePublicDiscourse.com* and *First Things*

"This book illuminates why the family is the pre-political basis of the state and shows us how the principles of Catholic social teaching raise up our political vision to a godly humanism, rooted in the image of God, and ordered to transcendent truth, beauty, and goodness. An indispensable guide for Catholic citizens."

— **C.C. Pecknold,** associate professor of theology,
The Catholic University of America

"White's book is a refreshingly balanced presentation of Catholic social teaching. Without pretending to be either a voting guide or a full theoretical treatise, it gives due regard to both social loves and aspects of social justice that were obscured by the political polarizations of the baby-boom generation."

— **F. Russell Hittinger,** PhD,
Warren Chair of Catholic Studies, University of Tulsa

RED, WHITE, BLUE, AND CATHOLIC

STEPHEN P. WHITE

Liguori

Imprimi Potest:
Stephen T. Rehrauer, CSsR, Provincial
Denver Province, the Redemptorists

Published by Liguori Publications
Liguori, Missouri 63057

To order, call 800-325-9521 or visit Liguori.org.

Library of Congress Cataloging-in-Publication Data

Names: White, Stephen P., author.

Title: Red, white, blue, and Catholic / Stephen P. White.

Description: First Edition. | Liguori: Liguori Publications, 2016.

Identifiers: LCCN 2015049678 (print) | LCCN 2015051380 (ebook)
      ISBN 9780764826450 | ISBN 9780764870774

Subjects: LCSH: Catholics—Political activity—United States. |
  Voting—Religious aspects—Christianity. | Catholic Church—Doctrines. |
  Christianity and politics—Catholic Church. | Christianity and politics—United States.

Classification: LCC BX1407.P63 W45 2016 (print) | LCC BX1407.P63 (ebook)
    DDC 261.7088/28273—dc23

LC record available at http://lccn.loc.gov/2015049678

Liguori Publications, a nonprofit corporation, is an apostolate of the Redemptorists. To learn more about the Redemptorists, visit Redemptorists.com.

Printed in the United States of America
20 19 18 17 16 / 5 4 3 2 1
First Edition

Contents

Foreword

Saint Thomas More was beheaded in 1535, at the age of fifty-seven. He had been lord chancellor of the British Empire, speaker of the House of Commons, a diplomat of the British crown, and a very popular and persuasive writer. Thomas More enjoyed a long career of civil service because of his reputation for fair-mindedness, integrity, and brilliance. But his integrity later cost him his life. When King Henry VIII defied the pope's authority, More tried to keep out of the dispute, but Henry forced his hand. When More refused to deny the Church's authority, he was executed.

Servant of God **Dorothy Day** was a bohemian anarchist, then an atheistic socialist. Day had an abortion in her twenties and believed she would be sterile after the procedure. When she found herself pregnant and gave birth to a daughter in 1926, she began a period of religious exploration. In 1927, she encountered Jesus in a personal way through a Catholic religious sister, Sr. Aloysia, SC. Day and her daughter, Tamar, were both baptized as Catholics within the year. As a Catholic, Dorothy Day became even more committed to social activism. She became an advocate for the rights of the poor, and at the same time a fierce critic of communism. She became an active evangelist. She started a newspaper, *The Catholic Worker*, and the Catholic Worker Movement. She was not always popular, and at times her judgments were mistaken, but from the moment of her conversion, she strove to be faithful and to build a civilization committed to the dignity of every human being.

Dr. Jerome Lejeune was a French geneticist. As a medical researcher, he was most comfortable in a scientific laboratory. It was in his laboratory that Lejeune discovered the genetic origins of Down syndrome in 1958, and from there the genetic roots of other chromosomal abnormalities. The chromosomal mapping Lejeune undertook pointed to new methods of treatment and care for those with disabilities. Unfortunately, his work also led to the prenatal diagnosis and abortion of those with genetic disabilities. Until his death in 1994, Lejeune dedicated his time, his finances, and his research to ending legal protection for abortion. His pro-life stance ostracized him from many in the scientific community, but he was a tireless defender of the unborn, the family, and the Gospel of Life.

Thomas More, Dorothy Day, and Jerome Lejeune were three very different people. On the surface, the statesman, the activist, and the scientist seem to have very little in common, but all three were serious disciples of Jesus Christ. And all three were public witnesses to the Gospel, to the profound importance of the family and the person, and to the transforming and saving power of divine grace. All three were good citizens, each in his or her own way.

More, Day, and Lejeune represent the vocation of all lay Catholics in the world. In its document On the Church in the Modern World (*Gaudium et Spes*), the Second Vatican Council said that laity are "bound to penetrate the world with a Christian spirit" and are "called to be witnesses to Christ in all things in the midst of human society." Every layperson, the Church says, should work for the "sanctification of the world," so that all spheres of human work and culture bring praise to Christ, the Redeemer.

To work for the sanctification of the world is to use our talents and gifts in every area of our lives so that they bring peace, joy, justice, and truth to the world. To be witnesses to Christ is to conduct ourselves in a way that is ordered to the profound truths of the Gospel. When we use our professional and personal lives to bring glory to God, the effects transform the lives of other people.

Jesus put things more simply. He gave the same command to all those who followed him: "Go, therefore, and make disciples of all nations" (Matthew 28:19). This is God's command to each one of us. Making disciples is not just the responsibility of priests, deacons, bishops, and religious brothers and sisters. Making disciples is your responsibility. And this means that Christ expects faithful Catholics to witness to the Gospel—no matter where we are, no matter what our profession, no matter how qualified or unqualified we judge ourselves to be. God gives us the command, and in our baptism he gives us the grace to carry out that command. We're equipped to be good witnesses because the Holy Spirit is with us. We can be prepared for this task with help from books like this one.

Part of Catholic witness is good citizenship: active and faithful participation in the life of our community. We make disciples in our own nation by forming just and charitable Christian communities. We often think of good citizenship in terms of voting or political participation. Those are important parts of the virtue of citizenship, but they aren't the only parts. Being a good citizen means treating the people in our communities as Jesus would. It means making choices that support the family, the unborn, and the poor. It means being engaged with our neighbors, our fellow believers, and our community leaders.

****

I have known Stephen White for nearly two decades. I came to know him especially well when he was a student at the University of Dallas, where I served as chaplain. Stephen is a careful, thoughtful, and faithful student of Catholic social teaching. He draws from the riches of the Church's teachings to make judgments about contemporary issues.

Red, White, Blue, and Catholic demonstrates what I know about Stephen White's work. This book will be a helpful guide for Catholics who want to have a full sense of what good citizenship is all about. It offers practical insights into the sanctification of the world, the formation of Christian culture. Every family and parish can benefit from what Stephen suggests.

The principles of Catholic social teaching are often divisive, and unfortunately our culture often portrays them in conflict with each other. In politics, the media draw a false divide between care for the unborn and the family, on the one hand, and care for the poor and marginalized, on the other. Blind partisanship on the part of Catholics reinforces these false notions. We're called to remedy them by the witness and work of our lives; we're called to demonstrate the unity and consistency of the Church's teachings; and we're called to protect the unborn, support the family, and commit to solidarity with the poor.

Each one of us is called to be a saint. And a part of holiness is the virtue of good citizenship: commitment to the common good. In each of our lives, good citizenship will take different shapes and different expressions. But if we're faithful followers of Jesus, our citizenship on earth will reflect the glory of citizenship in heaven. I pray that this book will help you become a good citizen, help you become holy, and help each one of us make disciples of all nations.

—*Bishop James Conley,*
Diocese of Lincoln, NE

Introduction

On the first Tuesday following the first Monday of November in even-numbered years, U.S. voters go to the polls to cast ballots for the men and women who will represent them in Congress. Every four years, we vote for a president. On any given Election Day, roughly a quarter of those going to the polls nationwide are Catholic. That's a lot of Catholic voters, as many as thirty-two million in 2012.

Yet being Catholic doesn't seem to make much of a difference in how we vote. Exit polls indicate that in every presidential election going back to 2004, Catholic voters favored whichever candidate the whole nation favored and by nearly identical margins. In 2012, Catholics voted for the Democratic candidate (Barack Obama) over his Republican challenger (Mitt Romney) by the very same margin as Americans in general: 50 percent to 48 percent. The two previous presidential elections tell the same story. When Barack Obama defeated John McCain in 2008 (53 percent to 46 percent), Catholic voters favored Obama (54 percent to 45 percent). When George W. Bush defeated John Kerry by 51 percent to 48 percent in 2004, Catholics voters favored Bush by 52 percent to 47 percent.[1]

Some people will tell you the Catholic vote has become a national bellwether. But you could just as easily say that the Catholic vote is, at least when it comes to electing a president, meaningless. In fact, if by some act of God, all thirty-two million ballots cast by Catholics in the 2012 election had been lost and uncounted, Barack Obama would still have won the

---

1 All polling data from Pew Forum. "How the Faithful Voted: 2012 Preliminary Analysis," November 7, 2012.

popular vote by precisely the same margin: 50 percent to 48 percent. It seems there is nothing distinctive at all about how U.S. Catholics vote.

It wasn't always this way. A generation ago, the Catholic vote was a decisive bloc in U.S. electoral politics. During the late nineteenth and early twentieth centuries, large-scale immigration from Catholic nations in Europe, such as Ireland, Germany, Italy, Poland, and Portugal, brought millions of lower- and middle-class Catholics to the United States. This new ethnic-urban Catholicism changed the shape of American politics. Catholics played a huge role in the rise of the labor movement in the early twentieth century and became a mainstay of the Democratic Party, especially in the large cities of the Northeast and across the rustbelt and upper Midwest. This way of being Catholic in the United States was captured most clearly in 1960, when nearly 80 percent of Catholic voters cast a ballot for a Massachusetts Democrat, giving John F. Kennedy a razor-thin victory over Richard M. Nixon, making him the first (and to date, only) Catholic to hold the nation's highest office.

That was a high-water mark for Catholic distinctiveness in U.S. politics. Since then, being Catholic has come to mean less and less in public life. Today, there are more Catholics in Congress than ever before. The vice president, the speaker of the House (not to mention four of the six previous speakers), and six of the nine justices on the Supreme Court are Catholic. But there is nothing distinctively Catholic about how Catholics in public life today execute the duties of their offices.

Over the past generation, social issues (primarily abortion but also embryonic stem-cell research, euthanasia, and now same-sex marriage) have held prominence in U.S. politics. The Republican Party became the *de facto* home for religious conservatives and defenders of traditional sexual morality, while a vocal majority of the Democratic Party has become strongly pro-abortion, at least at the national level.

In the late 1970s, Democrats commanded a huge majority in the House of Representatives. That majority has steadily eroded over the past thirty years. Democrats for Life of America (DFLA) recently argued that the precipitous decline in pro-life Democrats in the House of Representatives accounts almost entirely for this shift. By DFLA's counting, there were some 125 pro-life Democrats in the House of Representatives in 1977. As of the writing of this book in 2015, there were two Democrats in the House deemed sufficiently pro-life to earn an endorsement from their own party's pro-life wing. Just two.

The U.S. bishops have spoken in support of a whole host of policy measures that would seem to suggest an affinity for the Democratic Party: warnings about the limits of markets to produce just economic outcomes, concerns about economic inequality, opposition to the use of capital punishment, condemnation of health-care laws that leave millions vulnerable to crippling medical costs, and—most recently in Pope Francis' encyclical On Our Common Home (*Laudato Si'*)—an emphasis on our obligation to protect our common home from all manner of environmental exploitation and ecological degradation. But as pro-life Democrats themselves argue, their party's deep devotion to the abortion license has driven away millions of faithful Catholic voters.

One of the more telling trends in U.S. electoral politics over the last two decades, at least in presidential elections, is that while you can't tell much about how someone will vote based on their being Catholic, there is a strong correlation between how Americans vote and how frequently they attend religious services. This is true not only for Catholics but also for almost every Christian denomination. Polling by the Pew Research Center on Religion and Public Life shows that, going back to at least 2000, Catholics who attend Mass once weekly or more tend to vote for Republicans, while Catholics who rarely or never attend Mass tend to vote for Democrats.[1]

Although it has become increasingly easy to see the Democrats as the party of social and sexual libertinism, big government, and irreligion, Republicans have invited criticisms as the party of individualism, greed, and religious fundamentalism. These are generalizations, of course, but each contains some grain of truth. What's more, these political divisions have reached a point at which they become self-reinforcing, with each side trying to gain the advantage by outdoing the other in appealing to their base.

Most discussions of the way Catholics vote focus on hot-button issues that touch on clear and easy-to-identify Catholic teaching: abortion, marriage, religious liberty, the waging of wars, and so on. Each party touts its supposed bona fides on this or that moral issue. Democrats woo Catholic voters on issues of social justice like immigration, health care, and antipoverty measures (often with support from the United States Conference of Catholic Bishops [USCCB]). Meanwhile, Republicans woo Catholics with their opposition to abortion, same-sex marriage, and more recently, their defense of religious freedom (also with support from the USCCB). None of this, however, seems to make much difference.

At times, it can seem as though there are two Catholic Churches in the United States. One emphasizes social justice, often at the expense of traditional Church teaching, and the other shows deep concern about adhering to orthodoxy and traditional morality while remaining skeptical of using government as a principal means of social reform. The false divide between orthodox faith and social-justice work is pernicious, a sign of dysfunction in our politics and an obstacle to the evangelical witness of the Church in an era when it is desperately needed.

The Catholic vote has lost its distinctiveness. Today it is little more than an elusive and tantalizing prize that never seems to materialize in a decisive, distinctive way. Why is this? Why does our Catholic faith appear to make so little difference in how we Catholics fulfill our citizenship? Christ said the world would "know that you are my disciples, if you have love for one another" (John 13:35). But are we living our lives, building our communities, and exercising our citizenship in ways that would suggest we are followers of Christ?

Are we living lives, building communities, and exercising our citizenship in ways that suggest we are followers of Christ?

Too often, we try to fit Church teachings into our existing political and social divides instead of going through the much more difficult process of truly confronting and challenging our views. The results have been bad for both the Church and the country. Catholic social teaching has become, for many, a tool rather than an overarching vision of the right ordering of society in the light of revelation and reason. Rather than allowing the Church's wisdom to shape our lives as citizens, we allow our political commitments to shape or distort our understanding of the Church's social teaching. Our political divisions spill over into our own religious commitments, dividing Catholics within the Church along the same fault lines that mar our political culture.

I say all this neither to split the "political baby" by suggesting a moral equivalence between the platforms or policies of Republicans and Democrats nor to call for a pox on both their houses, as tempting as that may be. I say this because we Catholics need to do better, both as Catholics and as Americans.

Polling data and broad-stroke political narratives can tell us something about how Catholics exercise their citizenship on Election Day. And because voting trends can be measured and analyzed, they are an easy focal point for talking about Catholic citizenship. But most of how we live as Catholic citizens doesn't happen in a voting booth. Most of the ways in which we shape and are shaped by our nation happen elsewhere.

> **Most of how we live as Catholic citizens doesn't happen in a voting booth. Most of the ways in which we shape our nation happen elsewhere.**

In this book, we'll look at things a little bit differently. This book is a Catholic guide to faithful citizenship for every day of the year—not just Election Day.

Citizenship. That's a word that doesn't get used as much anymore, and it's a concept that is too-often neglected or at least understood narrowly. These days, we usually talk about citizenship in a legalistic way, with reference to particular rights and benefits. The Constitution and laws of the United States distinguish between the rights and benefits of citizens and noncitizens, which is entirely proper. One of the great responsibilities of the citizens of a democratic republic like ours is to shape the laws. That's a responsibility that is usually carried out by our elected representatives and so is tied to the right to vote, a right that belongs exclusively to citizens.

The fact is, most of us are citizens long before we are able to vote. Americans under the age of eighteen are not allowed to vote, but that doesn't mean they are exempt from the demands of good citizenship. Even those who lack legal citizenship—

recent immigrants, resident aliens, expatriates—can make important contributions to civic life. They may not be citizens, but they can fulfill most of the duties and reap many of the benefits of citizenship just the same. Citizenship, in its most important sense, is about participation and membership in a community. It's about belonging to a community, acting for the good of that community, taking responsibility for that community, loving that community, and teaching others to care for and love for it, too. Part of that task is accomplished by voting. But the far greater part, in fact almost everything we do, does not happen in a voting booth. It is in this richer understanding of citizenship and civic life that the Church's teachings about social justice make the most sense. Citizenship isn't a trophy or a prize. It's a work of love.

This book won't offer any grand stratagems for resolving the divisions that mark our nation's politics. If I had an easy answer to that, I'd be running for president, not writing this book. But what this book does aim to do is set our nation's political travails against the broader and deeper setting that the Church itself provides, to use the rich tradition of the Church and its social teaching to fill in some of the gaps that pockmark our nation's political discourse. And we'll look at some critical issues facing Catholic citizens, and yes, also Catholic voters.

This book, hopefully, will help restore a fuller sense of citizenship. This book is not intended to replace or compete with the many useful "Catholic voter guides" that have been issued over the years by various dioceses and Catholic organizations. Instead, this book aims to reconnect the Church's guidance for voting and the consideration and balancing of the many important issues facing our nation to the more every day, often neglected understanding of what it essentially means to be part of a political community.

At the heart of good citizenship is love, that is, love for the people and institutions to which we are bound by birth and by choice. This is not a blind love, which ignores failings and sins, but a love that wills and strives for the best for ourselves and for our country. In this light, it becomes easier to see why the best thing we can do as Americans is to become the best and most faithful Catholics we can be. Our Catholic faith needs to give us a new horizon and decisive direction in our lives, all parts of our lives.

This is a book written out of love for both Church and country. This is a book written to argue and defend what it presumes at the outset: that being a good citizen is an integral part of Christian discipleship and that the greatest contribution we can make as citizens is to live our Catholic faith wholeheartedly and without reserve. Instead of red-state Catholics and blue-state Catholics, we need Catholics who are in love with the United States and act out of the deepest traditions and convictions of their faith to make this country the best version of itself that it can be. We need Catholic citizens who are Red, White, Blue, and Catholic.

As this is a book about *Catholic* citizenship, the first chapter will look at how the Church understands society and our place in it through its social teaching. Although a bit theoretical, it's necessary to have a solid framework before we get into the nitty-gritty. Because this is also a book about Catholic *citizenship*, the following three chapters will look at some specific areas in which the Catholic understanding of citizenship and society is relevant.

In chapter 2, we'll look at the family, an institution that forms the bedrock of all society. As Pope John Paul II said, "As the family goes, so goes the nation and so goes the whole world in which we live."[2] In chapter 3, we'll look at the Church

---

2   Homily of Pope John Paul II. Perth, Australia, November 30, 1986.

and what it brings to civil society. These days, there are a great many questions about religious freedom and the place of religion in our public life. It is essential to understand that the freedom of the Church is not just for the sake of the Church and its members but also for the good of society. Without religious freedom, the common good suffers greatly. In chapter 4, we'll review a selection of other areas of social life that are crucial to the functioning and health of our society. From the workplace to the shopping mall, the way we live and the choices we make have enormous impacts on ourselves and those around us. In chapter 5, we'll examine the ways in which being Catholic shapes how we think about law and freedom. In chapter 6, we'll look at some practical steps each of us can take to live out our vocation as Catholic citizens.

CHAPTER 1

The Church and Modern Politics

U.S. politics can often seem like a tug of war between two irreconcilable ideological camps. One side wants more freedom for individuals and the market and less control by the state, while the other side wants more governmental control and less freedom for the market and individuals. This is an oversimplification, but it does describe a fundamental dynamic of U.S. politics. And that's a problem, because what's left out by these increasingly polarized accounts of what America's future should look like is the most important pillar of a healthy society.

The good news is that the Church's social teaching is a powerful tool that can help us understand how to fill that gap in our current political debates. Catholic social teaching is a key that, when understood in full, fits the lock of our troubled politics. The bad news is that the Church's social teaching is often only partially understood, ignored, or worse, used for partisan leverage in the tug of war that's at the heart of our polarized politics.

Before we look at how the Church's social teaching can help fill the gap in our politics, it's worth looking at a particular episode from the 2012 presidential campaign when this divide in U.S. politics was revealed with unusual clarity. As well, some of the basic issues that shape our differing views about the role of government and the nature of society rose to the surface during this time.

During a campaign stop in Virginia in July 2012, President Barack Obama spoke to a crowd about shared responsibility. He was trying to make a point about how much individual success depends on the success and hard work of those around us. The president's words set off a media firestorm: "If you've got a business, you didn't build that. Somebody else made that happen." [3]

In context, the president's words are rather benign. If someone else had said them, or if they had been uttered in a different time and place, they would have been unremarkable. But in July of 2012, the president's major economic initiatives—the 2009 stimulus, "Cash for Clunkers," the bailout of Detroit—were widely thought of as failures. The unemployment rate that month was higher than it was the day President Obama took office and had been over 8 percent for more than forty consecutive months.

So when the president suggested that someone other than entrepreneurs and business owners, like maybe government, was what really builds businesses and creates jobs, Republican nominee Mitt Romney pounced.

Romney called the president's words "insulting to every entrepreneur, every innovator in America." [4] The Romney campaign turned the president's words into a slogan symbolizing everything dubious about Obama's progressive vision of expansive government action. The Romney campaign's message was this: Democrats in general, and Barack Obama in particular, think government is the answer to every problem.

This tug of war between more government and less market and the party of more market and less state (put another way,

---

3   The White House. Office of the Press Secretary. "Remarks by the President at a Campaign Event in Roanoke, Virginia." July 13, 2012.

4   Gabriel, Trip, and Peter Baker. "Romney and Obama Resume Economic Attacks, Despite a Few Diversions." *New York Times*, July 17, 2012.

of the state versus the individual) is common. But we don't live our lives in isolated cocoons of autonomy. Neither do our lives center on government. So, why do our politics seem primarily concerned with these two alternatives? Is it any wonder that one of the most common complaints among U.S. voters is that politicians seem to be out of touch with the everyday realities of American life?

What both visions of government and politics largely miss, albeit in different ways, are those all-important spaces: families, churches, schools, unions, businesses, charities, fraternal organizations, and the like, where most of our lives actually happen. These are spaces where we are neither alone as individuals nor engaged directly with government.

As it happens, the social teaching of the Catholic Church has long been a defender of precisely these mediating institutions, which make up what we call *civil society*. The Church's social teaching offers a rich and compelling vision of the proper arrangement of society, one that protects and promotes the institutions that make up civil society (families, churches, schools, voluntary associations of all kinds) while also protecting the proper freedom of both individuals and civil society.

Four permanent principles make up the foundation of Catholic social teaching. We'll discuss each in turn and how they are related to one another. The Second Vatican Council's Pastoral Constitution on the Church in the Modern World (*Gaudium et Spes*) opens with these beautiful words:

> The joys and the hopes, the griefs and the anxieties of the men of this age, especially those who are poor or in any way afflicted, these are the joys and hopes, the griefs and anxieties of the followers of Christ. Indeed, nothing genuinely human fails to raise an echo in their hearts.

So we begin our discussion where the Church begins, with the dignity and vocation of the individual person, with all our joys and hopes, griefs, and anxieties. It's for the sake of the human person that civil society exists in the first place.

The Human Person and Civil Society

In his 1891 encyclical Of New Things (*Rerum Novarum*), which gave birth to what we now call Catholic social teaching, Pope Leo XIII criticized both socialism and what he called "liberalism," by which he meant a system in which economics are not circumscribed within a moral framework. If socialism wanted to place all human activity under the control of the state, liberalism made the opposite error, treating human beings as mere individuals and the societies and associations they form as no more than the sum of so many parts. The horrors of twentieth-century communism have made the dangers of socialism more obvious to us today, but the second error is very widespread in the United States and often goes unnoticed.

Against both the socialist and liberal views of society, Pope Leo offered a richer alternative. His argument was subtle and complex, drawing heavily on Scripture and tradition, especially the ideas of St. Thomas Aquinas. It saw human society as arising from the very nature and vocation of the *human person*—our natural affections for one another, our desire to form families, and to engage in common endeavors for the sake of ourselves, our families, and our neighbors. This was very different from socialist claims that human society could be remade by a bureaucratic state according to scientific principles. It was also very different from various liberal theories that made the autonomous will of the individual the principle by which human society would be organized.

Human beings are created by God. As we learn in the Book of Genesis, we are created in his image, which is the source of our human dignity. But we are also made for something, for communion with others in this life and for perfect communion with God in the next. For this reason, we are created free, not free to do as we please (Adam and Eve showed us how that turns out) but free to pursue the good for which we were created. Our freedom is for the sake of building communion, for building those relationships of love in which we are able to be most fully ourselves. The Church's vision of human society is built on this view of human nature.

The institutions of civil society should serve the human person.

Pope Leo understood this, which is why he insisted that the institutions of civil society serve the human person. The state, in turn, serves both civil society and the person. And while the state has primary responsibility for ensuring the common good, every person and every part of civil society has an obligation to the common good as well. Pope Leo writes in *Rerum Novarum*:

> "A brother that is helped by his brother is like a strong city" (Proverbs 18:19). It is this natural impulse which binds men together in civil society; and it is likewise this which leads them to join together in associations which are, it is true, lesser and not independent societies, but, nevertheless, real societies.

These real societies that make up civil society are necessary and good for human flourishing. They need to serve the common good, but that also means they need to be free to do so. Pope Leo continues:

For, to enter into a "society" of this kind is the natural right of man; and the State has for its office to protect natural rights, not to destroy them; and, if it forbid its citizens to form associations, it contradicts the very principle of its own existence, for both they and it exist in virtue of the like principle, namely, the natural tendency of man to dwell in society.

It is natural for men and women to form associations and enter into civil society. It's a fundamental part of what human beings do. When the state prevents this, or unnecessarily interferes, it is violating a fundamental human right, the very human rights the state exists to protect in the first place.

Pope John Paul II reiterated this point in his 1991 encyclical One Hundred Years (*Centesimus Annus*), which marked the 100th anniversary of Leo's *Rerum Novarum*. The Polish pope placed civil society at the center of his own reading of Pope Leo's encyclical and of the Church's entire social doctrine:

According to *Rerum Novarum* and the whole social doctrine of the Church, the social nature of man is not completely fulfilled in the State, but is realized in various intermediary groups, beginning with the family and including economic, social, political and cultural groups which stem from human nature itself and have their own autonomy, always with a view to the common good.

Civil society is the place where our social nature as human beings is realized. You could hardly ask for a clearer indication of just how important civil society is and why it is such a big problem that our politics so often overlook it.

Civil society is the place where our social nature as human beings is realized.

If all this seems rather abstract and confusing, consider the concrete example of a family, an example Pope Leo used himself. A man and woman come together, form a marriage bond as husband and wife, and start a family. They share responsibility for each other and for their children. Their obligations toward each other and their children come with certain corresponding obligations and rights. The rights and obligations of a husband to his wife are obviously different than the rights and obligations of a father toward his children. Parents have unique authority over their children. Children, in turn, owe their parents obedience and respect but also deserve the care and love of their parents.

All these intertwining relationships add up to more than the sum of their parts. A family is more than an arbitrary group of people of differing ages who happen to be genetically related and living together. A family is much more. We all recognize that. We even recognize it perhaps especially when things don't work out the way we know they should. When families break down, when spouses split, when parents neglect children, when children abandon parents, these situations strike us immediately as tragic, as failures, as something less than what should have been.

A family itself is a good thing, a true society that arises from natural human affections, serves the good of its members and society, and deserves the recognition, protection, and cooperation of others. We know all this as if by instinct (the Church would say by *nature*), so much so that we expect other people and even civil authorities to recognize it, too.

This is almost universally true, to the point at which even in the midst of the ongoing debate over same-sex marriage, both sides insist that marriage ought to be recognized by the state. The differing sides certainly disagree about what a marriage is, but they generally agree that when the state fails to recognize a marriage, it is committing an injustice, which is a big reason the debate elicits so much passion from both sides.

Notice, too, that the family is not a creature of the state. Our laws didn't invent the family, and law can't write it out of existence, at least not without a great deal of coercion and bloodshed. The family is vital to the flourishing of individuals and of society as a whole and so deserves the protection of law for the sake of its members, for its own sake, and for the sake of the common good.

The family is just one example of an institution that makes up the space we call civil society. The Church is another obvious example of an institution that deserves the protection and respect of the state but is not a creation of the state. The freedom of the Church isn't a concession the state makes to keep the peace, it's something the state owes to the Church. The Church reminds us that there are horizons beyond politics, higher standards of justice than human laws, and judgment beyond that of humans. The Church teaches us lessons that no human law ever could. Who but the Church can teach us to love God and neighbor as we ought? Where else will we learn civilizing lessons like the last shall be first, the strong must protect the weak, or that our dignity is rooted in the majesty of our divine Creator? All of these are things the Church does to shape citizens, to make us the kind of men and women capable of living our freedom well. And we haven't even mentioned the work the Church does for the poor, the homeless, the hungry, the elderly, the young, the abandoned, unwed mothers, and so forth. Through the Church, men and women offer worship to God, which is also a matter of justice, of giving to God what is due to him. Yes, the Church deserves to be free to fulfill its role in the life of society not just for its sake but also for the sake of society, just as the family deserves to be free to fulfill its role for the sake of society, too.

The continuing decline of the family in the United States and our more recent controversies over religious freedom are, in large part, crises of civil society. The government has had a role to play in each crisis coming about. No doubt, solutions to these challenges will involve government, law, and the courts, but the primary source of these problems, and the only hope for long-term solutions, lies in civil society.

Subsidiarity

Each of the myriad associations and institutions that make up civil society has a purpose to fulfill. So long as that purpose serves the good of its members and the common good, the institutions of civil society deserve the freedom to fulfill their purposes. It's part of the state's job to ensure them that freedom by ensuring that things are kept in order. Social order isn't just about ensuring laws aren't broken. It's about ensuring that the different parts of society are free to be what they are: that families are free to create and raise the next generation, that the Church is free to provide moral formation and religious sustenance, that businesses are able to create wealth and distribute goods and services, that schools educate, and so forth. Social order also means that the different institutions that make up society are using their respective freedoms responsibly. This idea is at the heart of another principle of Catholic social teaching: *subsidiarity*.

Subsidiarity is often taken to be a fancy word for keeping "Big Brother" off our backs. That's certainly part of it. Pope John Paul II made this point clearly in *Centesimus Annus* when he described subsidiarity:

> A community of a higher order should not interfere in the internal life of a community of a lower order, depriving the latter of its functions, but rather should support it in case of need and help to coordinate its activity with the activities of the rest of society, always with a view to the common good.

What this means is that subsidiarity is mostly about making sure every part of society, from the family on up to the state, is fulfilling its proper role and assisting other parts of society in fulfilling theirs. Subsidiarity is not just about exercising authority at the lowest possible level. It's about locating social responsibility in its proper place.

This means that subsidiarity can be violated when government intrudes into areas of life where it has no business sticking its nose. It also means that the institutions of civil society have an obligation to fulfill their social roles. Civil society has work to do, and we have work to do. When we fail in our responsibilities to one another—when the weak aren't being cared for, when children aren't being educated, when employers aren't caring for their workers—the slack has to be picked up by someone else. That someone else, for better or worse, is usually government.

When government starts taking on the work civil society ought to be doing, we get big problems. This isn't because government is bad. (The Church insists that government is both good and necessary.) It's because while government is good at some things, it's usually bad at the kinds of things civil society should be doing instead, like raising kids, looking after the moral and spiritual well-being of a congregation, or taking care of mom and dad in their old age. Government can easily supplant the role of civil society not because it's better at fulfilling that role, but because citizens like us grow used to having someone else do our work for us. Of course, we still often complain loudly when government does a poor job of the work we're supposed to be doing in the first place. Government, it turns out, is an easy scapegoat.

Solidarity

If subsidiarity is important for keeping responsibility within society, it is also important because a thriving civil society is essential for the development of *solidarity*. Solidarity is a sense of shared responsibility, that is, a sense that we're responsible to some degree for the well-being of all. More than a sense of responsibility, solidarity is a virtue, the habit of social cooperation for the good of others and the community. Without subsidiarity, civil society withers away. Without civil society, solidarity dies.

In his book *Reflections on the French Revolution* (1789), The Irish philosopher and statesman Edmund Burke famously described the role that civil society plays in forming citizens for responsible participation in society: "To be attached to the subdivision," he wrote, "to love the little platoon we belong to in society, is the first principle (the germ as it were) of public affections. It is the first link in the series by which we proceed towards a love to our country, and to mankind." Solidarity is born in civil society.

Think about where you first learned to be responsible, where you learned to share, to get along with people you found difficult, to protect the weak, and to ask and give forgiveness.

Think of where you learned empathy and the importance of honesty, the value of hard work, the importance of fairness and sacrifice, and the joy that comes from helping others. These are the lessons of solidarity. We can learn about these lessons from a book, but if solidarity is to become a habit of living rather than a vague ideal, we have to practice living these lessons. The virtue of solidarity is learned in our families, parishes, and schools. We learn it in the clubs we form, the charities we assist, the unions we join, and the neighbors we greet. The solidarity that arises from these institutions is a check both on a false sense of individualism and the encroachment of the state.

As Pope Benedict XVI wrote in his encyclical Charity in Truth (*Caritas in Veritate*): "The principle of subsidiarity must remain closely linked to the principle of solidarity and vice versa, since the former without the latter gives way to social privatism, while the latter without the former gives way to paternalist social assistance that is demeaning to those in need." As it happens, Theodore Roosevelt made an almost identical point more than 100 years earlier: "Voluntary action by individuals in the form of associations of any kind for mutual betterment or mutual advantage often offers a way to avoid alike the dangers of state control and the dangers of excessive individualism." [5]

Solidarity can reveal itself in our laws and in the priorities our government sets, but it is born in civil society. Solidarity doesn't trickle down from above. It wells up from the roots of society until it touches every level, including government.

---

5   Roosevelt, Theodore. "Christian Citizenship: Address before the YMCA, Carnegie Hall, NY." December 30, 1900.

The Common Good

There is one more principle of the Church's social teaching that needs to be highlighted: the *common good*. The common good is, to quote the Second Vatican Council, "the sum total of social conditions which allow people, either as groups or as individuals, to reach their fulfillment more fully and more easily" (*Gaudium et Spes*). It's more than that, though. The common good is *our good*, the good of all members of the human family. The common good is not some ideal collective opposed to the good of individual persons, nor is it the good of the majority, determined by utilitarian calculus of the greatest possible happiness for the greatest possible number of individuals. Rather, the common good includes the good of each individual, material as well as moral and spiritual. It is also the good of every institution of civil society, of the nation, and of all human society. It arises from the dignity of the human person, is made concrete through subsidiarity and solidarity, and is the fullest earthly expression of the communion for which we were created. It is, in short, the goal and measure of human society.

The common good includes the good of each individual, material as well as moral and spiritual.

One hears, from time to time, that government is a "necessary evil." Thomas Paine used this phrase in his famous pamphlet *Common Sense* in 1776. But like much of what Thomas Paine thought, it's not true. The Catholic Church certainly doesn't think so. Government exists for the sake of the common good. There's no question that governments can cause harm. It's difficult to find a single example in history of a government that wasn't up to some mischief or another. But government isn't defined by what it does wrong, or even by the evil it exists to prevent. The measure of government is the good that it serves, and government exists to serve the common good.

Every person and every level of society is responsible for the common good, but government is responsible for the common good in a particular way. In fact, government bears primary responsibility for the common good. Without the rule of law, without the proper distribution of public goods, without recourse to common defense, without assistance in times of distress, civil society would not be able to function as it ought. No other institution is capable of taking responsibility for the good of the nation as a whole.

American distrust of government runs deep, and insofar as it guards against abuses of political power, a certain skepticism toward the state is healthy. But deep suspicion of government as such, seeing political order as a necessary evil to be tolerated only begrudgingly, is foreign to Catholic social teaching. Such an aversion to government is also contrary to the vision of America's founders, who, in drafting the Constitution, expressed beautifully just what they hoped to preserve by so doing:

> We the People of the United States, in Order to form a more perfect Union, establish Justice, insure domestic Tranquility, provide for the common defense, promote the general Welfare, and secure the Blessings of Liberty to ourselves and our Posterity, do ordain and establish this Constitution for the United States of America.

Government exists because the very foundation of a free and flourishing society, our good and the good of us all, depends on it.

More Than a Theory

The Church's understanding of society is more than a theory. It describes an important and distinctive part of the way we Americans actually live our lives. From its birth, our country has been marked by an unusually robust and vibrant civil society, something those of us who have lived here all our lives can easily take for granted.

In 1840, a Frenchmen named Alexis de Tocqueville published his reflections on his travels through the still-young United States. His book, *Democracy in America,* offers an outsider's perspective of the habits and character of our country and its experiment in democratic self-government. One of the things that most struck him was the vitality and variety of American civil society. He wrote:

> Americans of all ages, all conditions, and all dispositions constantly form associations. They have not only commercial and manufacturing companies, in which all take part, but associations of a thousand other kinds, religious, moral, serious, futile, general or restricted, enormous or diminutive. The Americans make associations to give entertainments, to found seminaries, to build inns, to construct churches, to diffuse books, to send missionaries to the antipodes; in this manner they found hospitals, prisons, and schools. If it is proposed to inculcate some truth or to foster some feeling by the encouragement of a great example, they form a society. Wherever at the head of some new undertaking you see the government in

France, or a man of rank in England, in the United States you will be sure to find an association.

He also noted that, in a democratic republic like ours, these associations of civil society were more than a curiosity. They were vitally important to the health of the nation itself:

> If men who live in democratic countries had neither the right nor the taste to unite in political goals, their independence would run great risks, but they could preserve their wealth and their enlightenment for a long time; whereas if they did not acquire the practice of associating with each other in ordinary life, civilization itself would be in peril. A people among whom particular persons lost the power of doing great things in isolation, without acquiring the ability to produce them in common, would soon return to barbarism.

What was true when de Tocqueville visited America is still true today, both the importance of civil society and the peril that comes with its loss. If anything, the larger and more diverse a nation becomes, the more important civil society becomes. But civil society is also more difficult to maintain in a large and diverse nation. Solidarity requires more work, and subsidiarity faces more pitfalls.

One of the most important tasks for us as Catholic citizens is to dedicate ourselves to the vitality and flourishing of civil society. This is a role U.S. Catholics have excelled at historically, not only in our families and our parishes but also in the almost unbelievable network of universities, schools, hospitals, hospices, homeless shelters, adoption agencies, crisis pregnancy centers, food banks, businesses, worker houses, clubs, sodalities, and religious houses that have contributed so much and yet become so ingrained in American life that we easily take them for granted.

None of these things just happened. They were built through shared sacrifice and deep faith. They are a testament to the truth of the Church's social teaching, to the power of the subsidiary institutions of civil society to bring about solidarity. They are our heritage, as Americans and as Catholics. So it is our responsibility as Americans and as Catholics to grow them, strengthen them, and when necessary, defend them so they continue enriching the lives of future generations.

These four principles are what the Church calls the four permanent principles of Catholic social teaching. The terms themselves are less important than the human and social realities they describe. These four principles, understood together, form the skeleton of the Church's vision of society. Our task as citizens is to add meat to the bones.

CHAPTER

Family, Marriage, and the Cradle of Life

In the last chapter, we looked at the four permanent principles of Catholic social teaching: dignity of the human person, solidarity, subsidiarity, and the common good. Together, these principles give us the framework for the Church's vision of the right ordering of society, but they won't make a bit of difference unless they're made concrete in the lives of those who profess to live by them.

Primarily, this is the work of the laity. The Second Vatican Council's Decree on the Apostolate of the Laity (*Apostolicam Actuositatem*) puts it this way: "The effort to infuse a Christian spirit into the mentality, customs, laws, and structures of the community in which one lives, is so much the duty and responsibility of the laity that it can never be performed properly by others."

The world desperately needs what the Church has to propose—the Good News—and the role of Catholics everywhere is to ensure that that proposal is being made. In this, the commitment and resolve of lay men and women is indispensable.

The Church insists that it has no technical solutions to offer to particular economic and political challenges. As the *Catechism of the Catholic Church* puts it, "It is not the role of the Pastors of the Church to intervene directly in the political

structuring and organization of social life. This task is part of
the vocation of the lay faithful, acting on their own initiative
with their fellow citizens" (*CCC* 2442). The first and most
important place where the vocation of the lay faithful plays
out is the family. Family is often taken to be a private sphere,
separate from politics and public life. To some extent, this is
true. Family is a sacred space, in which new citizens are made
and formed. At its best, it is a place of security and safety.
Family is the womb of all society. And because of this, family is
of the utmost importance for the well-being of our country. It
is the first and most fundamental arena in which our work as
disciples and citizens is accomplished.

The Family Makes the Citizen

Nowhere is there a more powerful source of love and devotion
than in the family. The bonds of affection that exist between
spouses, and between parents and their children, are a source
of life's greatest happiness. The family is the basic cell of all
society and the first school of both citizenship and discipleship.
Strong families are society's greatest guarantee of stability and
continued flourishing, even in times of crisis.

At the same time, the breakdown of familial bonds
is among the most heartrending of human tragedies and
destructive to healthy society. As Pope John Paul II put it,
"As the family goes, so goes the nation and so goes the whole
world in which we live." [2] This is not simply a pious slogan. The
importance of family cannot be overstated.

If the family is the foundation of society and of
civilization itself, then the signs of our times are troubling.
The foundation is cracking. Without stable families, society is
like a house built on sand. In the words of the Second Vatican
Council, "The well-being of the individual person and of

human and Christian society is intimately linked with the healthy condition of that community produced by marriage and family" (*Gaudium et Spes*). The crisis of the family is not just a crisis for individuals. Insofar as all societies depend on the family for the formation and education of children, of new citizens, the crisis of the family affects the whole of society now and far into the future.

None of us chooses our families. We are born into a community of persons, all sinners, but hopefully loving, upright, and understanding. Family is the one place where we cannot avoid the inescapable limits of our own will and consent. When we come to see other people not as persons in their own right but as means toward our own end or as problems to be solved, we lose sight of their humanity. And we risk losing sight of our own. The realities of family life inoculate us against this. In the family, we have no choice but to take other persons as they are for better or worse. Our parents are ours, and we depend on them and (eventually) they depend on us. Our siblings are ours, and we depend on them and they depend on us for better or worse. In the family, we learn to live with others not only when it's easy but also when it's hard. We learn the difficult lesson that our relationships with other people are not reducible to our own wants and needs. We learn the limits of our own willfulness. We learn that some relationships—the deepest, strongest, most important relationships—are not built on our consent but on love. We learn the importance of vulnerability and of tenderness toward those who are vulnerable before us.

Every family has its own story. None is a mere statistic. We cannot reduce the moral and vocational drama that plays out in each of our own lives and families to a series of generalizations and statistics. That said, we also have to be aware of the trends in modern marriage and family life.

Family stability goes hand in hand with marital stability, and on this front, the news is not encouraging. Rates of marriage in the United States have fallen as more young people are choosing to cohabitate rather than marry. Marriage is increasingly seen as the culmination of a sexual relationship rather than its starting point. Extensive research by W. Bradford Wilcox, who directs the National Marriage Project at the University of Virginia, shows marriage collapsing most dramatically among those who never finish high school (for whom births out of wedlock are highest), while those who finish college are the least likely to have a child outside of marriage.

Stable marriages are closely linked to economic prospects for children. Marriage, it turns out, is just about the most effective poverty deterrent we know of and yet it's being abandoned most rapidly by those who are already at an economic disadvantage. Forty percent of children born in the United States today are born to unmarried parents. For mothers younger than age thirty, the percentage spikes to over 50 percent. As *The New York Times* put it in 2012, "It used to be called illegitimacy. Now it is the new normal." [6]

Rates of marriage within the Catholic Church have also plummeted. The Center for Applied Research in the Apostolate estimates that, while Catholics make up about 25 percent of the U.S. population, only about 7 percent of marriages in the United States take place within the Catholic Church. [7] The implications of this are grave. Catholic families, like all families, aren't just struggling—they're not even starting.

---

6   DeParle, Jason, and Sabrina Tavernise. "For Women Under 30, Most Births Occur Outside Marriage." *New York Times,* February 17, 2012.

7   Gray, Mark M, ed. "Divorce (Still) Less Likely Among Catholics," 1964 blog CARA, September 26, 2013.

Although every Catholic in the United States is aware of a decline in the number of men being ordained to the priesthood—the number of priests being ordained every year in the U.S. has dropped 38 percent since 1970—what might be shocking is that the number of Catholic marriages has dropped 64 percent over the same period. As Timothy Cardinal Dolan put it, the *real* vocations crisis in the U.S. is marriage: "We have a vocation crisis to lifelong, life-giving, loving, faithful marriage. If we take care of that one, we'll have all the priests and nuns we need for the Church." [8]

Sadly, as the crisis in the family has become more evident, the family itself has become a political football. What was uncontroversial only a few short years ago now sounds to many ears like a politically charged, even partisan statement. The family, founded on the marriage of man and woman, is the most fundamental cell of all human society. How bizarre that family and marriage have become controversial! Human society has always been shaped by two fundamental, indisputable facts about human life: There's only one way to make new human beings, and new human beings are utterly incapable of caring for themselves and need someone else to care for them. These basic realities remain today, yet the natural institutions that have always guarded these relationships have suddenly become a matter of heated public debate. None of us would exist without a mother and a father, a fact which remains true even when human relationships break down in all the painful ways we know they can. Yet our culture often treats this fact as irrelevant.

If personal experience and the overwhelming cultural evidence doesn't convince you that the family is in crisis, then

---

8   "Archbishop Dolan: Marriage Is the 'Real Vocation Crisis.'" *Catholic World News,*
    August 13, 2009.

consider that the crisis in the family has reached such global proportions that, for the second time in a generation, an Ordinary General Synod of Bishops met in Rome to address challenges facing the family.

The Family as the Font of Civil Society

Of course, the family is not just a place for the *making* of children; it's where little tyrants (and we all start out as tyrants, adorable little bundles of willfulness) are shaped and formed into responsible men and women. The family is where we are first nourished and fed, where we learn right from wrong, where we learn to put others before ourselves, where we learn self-control, where we first learn to love God and cherish others, and where we learn about just punishment and mercy and forgiveness. Family is where we learn that the strong must defend the weak and that love covers a multitude of sins. Family is where we learn from experience our fundamental obligation to solidarity. If we don't learn these things from our families, where will we learn them? Our families shape and form the men and women we will become more than any other influence.

In this sense, our nation—every nation—is almost entirely dependent on the family for the formation and education of each new generation of citizens. If families are failing, that is, not just struggling but falling apart, then the nation has a deep problem.

Our laws can make life easier for families around the margins. Economic burdens have been a source of strife from time immemorial, which means that virtually everything the government does that affects economic policy, from labor and wage laws, to job training programs, to family tax preferences, to education policy and school choice, affects the financial stability of families. As Pope Francis reminded us over and over in *Laudato Si'*, "Everything is connected." But there is little the government can do directly to build strong families. The state doesn't deal in love and affection. We can't simply pass a law making men good fathers and faithful husbands. No legislator, by the stroke of his or her pen, can make a troubled family into a place of security, fidelity, and virtue rather than strife and division.

Marriage Makes the Family

The impact of law on marriage culture is mostly indirect, but there are some exceptions. Liberal divorce laws, including no-fault divorce, have been weakening the institution of marriage for decades. The recent redefinition of marriage by the Supreme Court in *Obergefell et al. v. Hodges, Director, Ohio Department of Health, et al.* (No. 14–556) has enshrined in U.S. law an understanding of marriage that is, from the point of view of every civilization in history, deeply inadequate because it deliberately denies the essential connection between marriage and the begetting and rearing of children in order to make room for same-sex couples. But the redefinition of marriage by the Supreme Court is not the cause of the challenges facing the family in the United States. It's more a symptom of a culture in which marriage is seen as exclusively pertaining to the personal gratification of those entering into marriage. The begetting and rearing of children is becoming seen as, at most, an optional feature of marriage with no connection to the essence of the institution.

This change in how our culture sees marriage is due in large part to the separation of sex and marriage that was fueled by the sexual revolution and catalyzed by the contraceptive pill. If sex is separated from children, it was only a matter of time before marriage became separated from the idea of family. As the Second Vatican Council put it in *Gaudium et Spes*: "Marriage and conjugal love are by their nature ordained toward the begetting and educating of children. Children are really the supreme gift of marriage and contribute very substantially to the welfare of their parents." Separate marriage from the begetting and educating of children, and the welfare of the parents suffers, as does the welfare of society as a whole.

One can have lots of sex and babies without marriage. This, of course, has always been the case, but today it's becoming the new normal. Marriage is increasingly seen as being about the personal fulfillment of the two people who enter into it. No one seems to deny that marriage is good for the people getting married, but what purpose does marriage have once it is no longer considered the proper setting for sexual intimacy? Why should we see marriage as the proper place for sexual intimacy when that behavior has been uncoupled, so to speak, from any necessary connection to raising kids? As far as U.S. law is concerned, marriage has been reduced to a vehicle for certain tax benefits and visitation rights. By redefining marriage, the Supreme Court has created a society in which a civil union is available to anyone who wants one, but nowhere does the state recognize the union of a man and a woman for the sake of raising the next generation as a privileged and natural institution. All of which poses the question: If marriage is no longer a natural and privileged institution dedicated to raising the next generation, what is it for?

We are in uncharted territory where marriage is concerned. For all the variety in sexual morality and marriage laws throughout human history, no civilization has ever separated marriage from children. Marriage has always been primarily concerned with the next generation, or it was until now. We live in a civilization and a culture that deny any moral limit on sexual behavior (apart from consent), aggressively deny the plainly obvious fact that human reproductive organs are in some primary way for the sake of reproduction, all while going to extraordinary lengths to make sure that the newest technology for stymieing the natural reproductive capacity of our bodies is made as widely available as possible. Openness to life within marriage is countercultural. It is also one of the most powerful, striking ways of witnessing to the truth about marriage, family, and the dignity of the human person. Having lots of kids doesn't make you a good Catholic, but marriage and family are more than just accessories to self-fulfillment. They are a vocation.

Marriage and family are more than just accessories to self-fulfillment. They are a vocation.

For Catholic spouses, there is an urgent need for greater formation before marriage and greater support after marriage. Marriage is a vocation—a mission. Beginning in late 2014, Pope Francis dedicated his Wednesday audiences to a catechesis on the family. In one address, he spoke of the three expressions that are essential to every marriage: "please," "thank you," and "I'm sorry." These simple words are not only important to everyday domestic tranquility but also reflect the way in which family life reflects our relationship with our heavenly Father. We ask for blessing (as in the Lord's Prayer), we give thanks (especially in the Eucharist), and when we fail, we ask forgiveness (especially in the sacrament of penance).

A healthy spiritual life and a healthy marriage reinforce one another. It's very important for Catholic couples to understand the deep connection between these two aspects of life.

Catholics parents must take seriously their role as primary educators of their children. It is not enough to outsource the formation of our children's character to schools, even the best Catholic schools. This is also a challenge for me as a father. How can I, as a Catholic parent, expect my child to learn what I am not willing to teach by word and example? How can I expect my child to grow deeply in the faith if I teach by example that an hour at Mass every week fulfills my religious obligation to God, who is the source of all that I am and have? How can I expect my children to make their faith the top priority and focal point of their lives if I don't? How can my children learn honesty if I do not insist on honesty or if I am not honest myself? How can they learn to ask forgiveness if they never see me ask for it or give it? How can they learn to trust authority if I am untrustworthy in my own authority? The same goes for a multitude of virtues, from the mundane such as cleanliness, punctuality, hard work, and patience, to the cardinal virtues of courage, prudence, self-restraint, temperance, and treating others with justice.

Family and marriage are not simply religious issues. They matter deeply to all society. Our common good depends on them. As Catholics, we have to defend these institutions not only for religious reasons (although those should be reason enough) but also for the sake of everyone. Objections to the way marriage and family are treated in our society cannot be dismissed as religious opinion. Society depends on the health of marriage and the family, and you don't have to read Scripture or listen to the pope to understand why.

The Gift of Our Humanity

What the Church has to say about the ordering of society begins with and flows from the dignity of the human person. Every human life is precious. Every human life comes into existence with a mother and a father. Every new human life arrives in this world utterly incapable of caring for itself, utterly dependent on the help and protection of others. Abortion destroys all this, because it is a refusal to submit to the "givenness" of family life. To choose abortion is to insist that we have ultimate power, including control of life and death, over precisely those persons whose profound vulnerability cries out for our protection and aid. When the immutable fact of family collides with the assertion, "I did not choose you. I have no responsibility for you," family ceases to be the place where the strong protect the weak and becomes a place where the strong exercise the power of life and death over the weak and innocent. Abortion is antithetical to family.

Nothing is more corrosive to the family, and thus to society, than the systematic eradication of unwanted lives. Although it remains rare in the United States, recent years have seen a growing push for the legalization of euthanasia, which, in the name of a false compassion, perpetuates the lie that some human lives are not worth living. When this lie is enshrined in law, when abortion and euthanasia are protected in law as "rights," it makes a mockery of human law, human rights, and freedom itself.

The dignity of human life must never be sacrificed on the altar of false freedom. Our human dignity from who and what we are, because of the One who made us and for whom we are destined, is not subject to consent, neither ours nor anyone else's. No one can have a right to take an innocent life. As Pope John Paul II wrote in The Gospel of Life (*Evangelium Vitae*):

To claim the right to abortion, infanticide and euthanasia, and to recognize that right in law, means to attribute to human freedom a perverse and evil significance: that of an absolute power over others and against others. This is the death of true freedom: "Truly, truly, I say to you, everyone who commits sin is a slave to sin" (John 8:34).

Yet how many Catholics support these evils with a false sense of compassion? How many of us have grown indifferent in the face of a hostile culture? How many times have we heard that abortion and other "social issues" are divisive, that the culture wars are bad for America, as though peace and justice could be achieved through our silence? How many Catholics have ignored the clear and unambiguous words of the bishops from November 7, 1989: "No Catholic can responsibly take a 'pro-choice' stand when the 'choice' in question involves the taking of innocent human life?"

Abortion has destroyed tens of millions of lives. It has poisoned our politics and dulled our moral sensibilities as a nation. Abortion has coarsened the soul of our nation. We cannot be silent. We must insist no one is disposable! No one can be thrown away.

We must also resist the temptation to see abortion as one issue among many. It's certainly true that there are other challenges facing our nation besides abortion. And it is true that the evil of abortion is linked in many ways to other social challenges, including poverty, racism, materialism, and consumerism. But if justice is to mean anything at all, if human dignity is anything more than a slogan, then it must insist on the defense of innocent life. Pope John Paul II made this point explicitly in *Evangelium Vitae*: "Laws which legitimize the direct killing of innocent human beings through abortion or euthanasia are in complete opposition to the inviolable right to life proper to every individual; they thus deny the equality of everyone before the law." To speak of social justice, human rights, or a preferential option for the poor while accepting abortion is profoundly incoherent and undermines justice itself.

During his 1987 visit to the United States, Pope John Paul II insisted that the greatness of America is built on a respect for the dignity of the human person. When that foundation erodes, so does any hope for American greatness: "This is the dignity of America, the reason she exists, the condition for her survival— yes, the ultimate test of her greatness: to respect every human person, especially the weakest and most defenseless ones, those as yet unborn." Abortion doesn't just threaten individual human lives. It puts the common good in jeopardy.

The numbers have reached such proportions that they are almost unimaginable. Since the Supreme Court legalized a right to abortion in 1973, some fifty-eight million lives have been snuffed out through legal abortion. That number is so huge it's hard to grasp. For comparison, the 100 largest cities in the United States have a combined population of almost sixty million as measured by the 2010 census. What is a faithful citizen to do in the face of injustice of such magnitude? The U.S. bishops, under the auspices of the USCCB, have identified four areas in which we can work to defend life. [9]

First, we all need to work to educate ourselves and others about the sanctity of human life. Public information and education programs are needed "to deepen understanding of the sanctity of human life and the humanity of unborn children, the moral evil of intentionally killing innocent

---

9   United States Conference of Catholic Bishops. "Pastoral Plan for Pro-Life
     Activities: A Campaign in Support of Life."

human beings—whether at the beginning of life or at its end—and the mission of the Church to witness to and serve all human life." [10]

Second, we have to work to care for women facing difficult or unwanted pregnancies. When faced with an unwanted pregnancy, the fear of rejection, pain, or shame, a financial burden or diminished career prospects, or the fear of raising a child in profoundly difficult circumstances, we know that many women are driven to choose abortion because it seems their only option. Our compassion and care for women who choose abortion must be as strong as our insistence that the new life they carry is not just a problem to be solved. The same commitment to protecting the dignity of the human person also compels us to stand with those who have aborted their own children.

This care must extend to the disabled, the sick, and the dying as well. Death and suffering are part of life. At the heart of our faith is the knowledge that Christ came not to eliminate suffering and death, but to conquer them, transforming them into the means of our salvation. We can and must strive to be witnesses to this Good News. In recent times, there has been an increasing awareness that witnessing to the dignity of all human life should limit our use of the death penalty to those cases in which the safety of society itself is in danger. As the *Catechism* puts it:

> Today, in fact, as a consequence of the possibilities which the state has for effectively preventing crime, by rendering one who has committed an offense incapable of doing harm—without definitely taking away from him the possibility of redeeming himself—

---

10 *Ibid*

the cases in which the execution of the offender is an absolute necessity "are very rare, if not practically nonexistent" (*CCC* 2267).

Protecting human life, even the lives of those guilty of terrible crimes, is a powerful witness to the sanctity and dignity of all human life, and a reminder that we ought not make ourselves masters over life and death.

A third approach to protecting life involves public policy. We, as Catholic citizens, must work to ensure the legal protection of the unborn as well as those faced with the question of assisted suicide. Just making laws is not enough. We must work to provide alternatives to those who are suffering.

This kind of assistance implicates public policy, but it also implicates us as individuals and families. Men and women who open their homes to children who might otherwise have been aborted; the tireless work of those in medical fields and hospice care; those who volunteer their time and talents to provide shelter and assistance for expectant mothers; and those who visit the imprisoned, including those on death row, are examples of Christians giving concrete witness to the dignity of human life. We should all ask ourselves: Have I sought ways to give similar witness, or have I been content to leave this task of discipleship to others?

Finally, the simplest and most important way to promote a culture of life is to pray. The work of salvation is accomplished not by us but by God. As our bishops have said:

> Prayer is the foundation of all that we do in defense of human life. Our efforts—whether educational, pastoral, or legislative—will be less than fully fruitful if we do not change hearts and if we do not ourselves overcome our own spiritual blindness. Only with

prayer—prayer that storms the heavens for justice and mercy, prayer that cleanses our hearts and our souls—will the culture of death that surrounds us today be replaced with a culture of life. [11]

We must also refuse to accept the unacceptable. Resignation in the face of great evil is tantamount to despair, a great sin. One day, we will each have to give an account of what we did, publicly and privately, to defend innocent life in our communities. We must not let our answer be silence.

---

11 *Ibid*

CHAPTER  3

Bringing Truth to Civil Society

We've discussed the ways in which the family is the foundation of society and the cradle of citizenship. We've discussed how strong families and marriages are threatened by, and the antidote to, what Pope Francis often describes as a "throwaway culture" and what Pope St. John Paul II called the "culture of death." These in turn are both connected to what Pope Benedict XVI called the "dictatorship of relativism," where our concept of freedom becomes untethered from the truth about the human person. This relativism, rather than leading to tolerance and peace, makes reconciliation impossible because there is no common ground. Pope Francis extended this point in his encyclical *Laudato Si'* to show how driving a wedge between freedom and truth has terrible consequences that extend to all of society, indeed to all of creation. It's worth citing him at length from that encyclical:

> The culture of relativism is the same disorder which drives one person to take advantage of another, to treat others as mere objects, imposing forced labor on them or enslaving them to pay their debts.... This same "use and throw away" logic generates so much waste, because of the disordered desire to consume more than what is really necessary. We should not think that political efforts or the force of

law will be sufficient to prevent actions which affect the environment because, when the culture itself is corrupt and objective truth and universally valid principles are no longer upheld, then laws can only be seen as arbitrary impositions or obstacles to be avoided.

If our situation is so grave and the disease so widely spread, what can be done, apart from individual efforts to live in a way that cuts against the grain of the prevailing culture? Part of the answer, it seems, is to recognize the limits of "top-down" solutions. Top-down solutions address symptoms rather than the problem itself. Law and politics have a limited ability to address these problems and their roots, so while they're necessary they aren't the solution. The cradle of citizenship and culture—marriage and family—and those myriad spaces of civil society where our common lives happen will have to be transformed. This is a tall order.

Those spaces of civil society where our common lives happen will have to be transformed.

It is perhaps a small consolation, given the magnitude of the challenge, to recognize that the transformation of everyday life is *always* the challenge facing Christians. And although the particular challenges of our time and place are new, such transformations have happened in the past. Western civilization was not an accident but an accomplishment.

The transformation of everyday life is always the challenge facing Christians.

The Church will play a decisive role in this herculean endeavor. The Church is both a source of solidarity (not only social solidarity but also real communion through time and space) and a guide. We are pilgrims on a journey. God knows we can't travel the road alone. Through the Church, our guide and mother, God ensures that we have the companionship, guidance, and grace necessary for our task. His grace is sufficient.

Religious Freedom

There is a limit to what human laws can do to make good citizens. We need something else to ensure that the freedom guaranteed by law does not devolve into license and end up harming citizens and the republic itself. In the United States, the Christian faith has always been that something. Our nation is a Christian nation, not in law, but in its foundation. Our country's dedication to religious freedom, like our dedication to human rights, has Christian roots. Without strong Christian communities, we may begin to lose sight of those founding dedications.

John Adams famously wrote that, "Our Constitution was made only for a moral and religious people. It is wholly inadequate to the government of any other." The point is not that there should be a religious test for citizenship or that priests and ministers should write our laws. Rather, Adams' point was simply this: Our laws alone cannot make citizens good. The better the citizens, the freer those citizens can be.

Charles Carroll, one of America's Founding Fathers and the only Catholic to sign the Declaration of Independence, said much the same thing:

> Without morals a republic cannot subsist any length of time; they therefore, who are decrying the Christian religion, whose morality is so sublime and pure...and insures to the good eternal happiness, are undermining the solid foundation of morals, the best security for the duration of free governments.

Perhaps the most famous defense of the importance of religion to the good of the nation was made by George Washington, who, in his Farewell Address in 1796, argued that the moral character necessary for a healthy democracy was made possible only by religion:

> Of all the dispositions and habits which lead to political prosperity, religion and morality are indispensable supports. In vain would that man claim the tribute of patriotism, who should labor to subvert these great pillars of human happiness, these firmest props of the duties of men and citizens. The mere politician, equally with the pious man, ought to respect and to cherish them. A volume could not trace all their connections with private and public felicity. Let it simply be asked: Where is the security for property, for reputation, for life, if the sense of religious obligation desert the oaths which are the instruments of investigation in courts of justice? And let us with caution indulge the supposition that morality can be maintained without religion. Whatever may be conceded to the influence of refined education on minds of peculiar structure, reason and experience both forbid us to expect that national morality can prevail in exclusion of religious principle.

It wasn't only the founding generation that understood the importance of religion. The history of our nation bears this out. Religion has always been an irreplaceable pillar of U.S. citizenship. Martin Luther King, Jr. understood this when he wrote from a Birmingham jail of "the most sacred values in our Judeo-Christian heritage," and "those great wells of democracy which were dug deep by the founding fathers in their formulation of the Constitution and the Declaration of Independence."

This is why we need religious freedom in this nation: Because our laws, all human laws, are insufficient to create or keep a society that is both free and virtuous unless citizens recognize and revere an authority greater than human law. Religion provides this, and so it is protected not only for the sake of religion but also for the sake of our nation, which cannot flourish without it.

If this seems a little backward, that's probably because it is a view of religious freedom that has fallen out of favor in recent decades and especially in the last few years. Today, religion is often seen as something to be tolerated by the government rather than a necessary precondition of good government. The right to religious freedom has come to be seen as a concession by the state to the personal autonomy and consciences of the people.

We must insist, with both the Church and the best of U.S. political traditions to support us, that religious freedom is good not only for believers who are in the minority but also for the nation as a whole. Religious freedom and civil society stand or fall together, and so religious freedom and the common good flourish or fail together. If the Church is not welcome to fulfill her role in society—materially, spiritually, morally, culturally— the Church and Christians will suffer. The greater damage, however, will be done to the nation as a whole, which will be deprived of the "firmest props of the duties of men and citizens."

But we shouldn't think that the Church's place in civil society begins and ends in the realm of ideas. Far from it!

In a 2013 interview which helped set the tone for his papacy, Pope Francis told the Italian Jesuit Antonio Spadaro that the Church's moral teachings have to be presented in their proper context if they are to take root in the rocky soil of our modern world. "The church's pastoral ministry," the Holy Father said, "cannot be obsessed with the transmission of a disjointed multitude of doctrines to be imposed insistently."

He went on, "Proclamation in a missionary style focuses on the essentials, on the necessary things: this is also what fascinates and attracts more, what makes the heart burn, as it did for the disciples at Emmaus."

The symphony of truth that the Church proclaims to the world is more than a list of do's and don'ts. If the Gospel is to be proclaimed effectively, it must be presented in its fullness. Very often we can be like the rich young man in the Gospel of Matthew, asking, "What good must I do to gain eternal life?" (Matthew 19:16). The question itself is fair enough. We ought to keep sight of our goal, which is eternal life with God. But the question easily becomes: "What's the minimum, the least that is required of me to get to heaven?"

Following the rules is important. Christ himself tells us, "If you love me you will keep my commandments" (John 14:15). But by focusing only on the Church's moral teachings, we can miss the forest of Christian discipleship for the trees of moral righteousness. As Pope Benedict XVI wrote in God Is Love (*Deus Caritas Est*), in a passage Pope Francis is fond of quoting, "Being Christian is not the result of an ethical choice or a lofty idea, but the encounter with an event, a person, which gives life a new horizon and a decisive direction."

The disciples on the road to Emmaus came to understand this in their encounter with the risen Christ, the Lord's revelation to them of the meaning of Scripture, and their recognizing him in the breaking of the bread. Their encounter with Christ transformed and inspired them. And it gave their lives a new horizon and a decisive direction. In short, it placed all that Christ had taught them about how to live well into the proper context, the truth about who Jesus Christ really is and why he came to save us. This has been a central theme of Pope Francis' pontificate. It's not a new theme, but Pope Francis seems to have found a way to convince the world of the freshness, the "fragrance of the Gospel," as he likes to call it.

In his first homily after his election as bishop of Rome, Pope Francis told his fellow cardinals that for all the good works the Church does, we must never lose sight of its primary mission, which is to proclaim Christ to the world for the salvation of souls: "We can walk [with others] as much as we want, we can build many things, but if we do not profess Jesus Christ, things go wrong. We may become a charitable NGO, but not the Church, the Bride of the Lord."

The Church works for the good of society. It feeds the poor, gives drink to the thirsty, clothes the naked, visits the imprisoned, shelters the homeless, comforts the sick, buries the dead, and does much more besides.

Pope Francis even took it a step farther. "When we do not profess Jesus Christ," he warned, "we profess the worldliness of the devil, a demonic worldliness." The Church works for the good of society. It always has and it always will. The Church feeds the poor, gives drink to the thirsty, clothes the naked, visits the imprisoned, shelters the homeless, comforts the sick, buries the dead, and does much more besides. But as Pope Francis reminds us, it is not its social work that makes the Church what it is. And if the Church becomes nothing more than an institution that fights against material poverty and worldly suffering, then the devil wins.

Why? Because the difference between the Church and every other philanthropist, humanitarian, and do-gooder in history is that the Church offers a share in the life of the risen Christ. Eternal communion with God is the great gift the Church offers the world. If it withholds that gift, even from a well-intentioned desire to alleviate the suffering of others, then the Church withholds its greatest treasure. The Church fails to give the world the one thing it alone can give.

The difference between the work of the Church and the work of an NGO (nongovernmental organization) or a social worker is immeasurable. Pope Francis continues: "We have to find a new balance; otherwise even the moral edifice of the church is likely to fall like a house of cards, losing the freshness and fragrance of the Gospel. The proposal of the Gospel must be more simple, profound, and radiant. It is from this proposition that the moral consequences then flow."

The Church's work of evangelization and its contribution to the good of society are inseparably connected.

Pope Francis was not suggesting that the Church's moral teachings are flimsy and unfounded, but that they can seem flimsy and disconnected when they become separated from their foundation in fullness of the Gospel. And when the

Church's moral teachings—which include the Church's social teaching—seem disconnected and flimsy, what reason do people have to listen to the Church? Why would anyone follow a set of arbitrary, flimsy, disconnected rules? Pope Francis doesn't want to jettison the Church's moral teachings. He wants to remind people of the deep and solid foundations on which those moral teachings rest, foundations which give those teachings their strength and make them compelling.

The Church's work of evangelization and its contribution to the good of society are inseparably connected. The Church cannot convey the fullness of the truth unless it acts—unless those of us who have been joined to Christ through our baptism make his love and mercy present in a world that longs for love and mercy.

Chances are, your parish and diocese are home to more Catholic aid organizations than you know. And chances are they could use a hand.

There are almost 17,500 parishes in the United States, more than 5,000 Catholic elementary schools, 1,200 high schools, and 225 Catholic colleges and universities. The nation's 549 Catholic hospitals served almost ninety million patients in 2014. In that same year, Catholic Charities—the largest private network of social service providers in the country—provided $3.7 billion in services for more than nine million people. There are hundreds upon hundreds of Catholic organizations, from international giants like the Knights of Columbus and the Society of St. Vincent de Paul to the tiny mutual aid societies, sodalities, and charitable and volunteer organizations that can

Red, White, Blue, and Catholic

be found in every Catholic parish across the country. Catholics run soup kitchens, hospice care centers, child care centers, free clinics, crisis pregnancy centers, adoption services. The list is almost endless. The Catholic Church's legacy of social aid and charitable work—of building a flourishing civil society—should be a point of pride for every Catholic.

It should also be a shared work. Chances are, your parish and diocese are home to more Catholic aid organizations than you know. And chances are, they could use a hand.

CHAPTER

The Economy

We haven't yet said anything about economics, although the Church's social teaching has a lot to say about the matter, and economic concerns play a large role in the decisions we make as citizens, both in our everyday lives and as voters. We'll focus on three aspects of the Church's teachings on economics: the first is what's called the *universal destination of material goods*; the second, which flows from the first, is a *preferential option for the poor*; and the third is about *capitalism and free markets*.

Everything we have is a gift: our lives, our talents, our intelligence, our families and friends, even the earth itself. God gave us these gifts for the sake of our happiness. This means that we are free to use the things of this world for our own benefit, but we also have an obligation to use them for the good of others and in service to the common good. To put it simply, everything we have is given to us so that we can serve others. This is the lens through which the Church understands and defends private property, wealth creation, and business activity. It is the same grounds on which it asserts that certain public goods—clean water, security, aid in time of emergency, and so forth—be distributed equitably as a matter of justice. And it is on these grounds that the Church insists those who enjoy material wealth have an obligation to use that wealth for the good of others. Our private property is ours so that we can use it to serve others. That's an understanding of property and wealth that is decidedly countercultural, but it has been the Church's understanding of wealth since its beginnings.

The Second Vatican Council makes this point clearly in *Gaudium et Spes*: "In using them, therefore, man should regard the external things that he legitimately possesses not only as his own but also as common in the sense that they should be able to benefit not only him but also others." A few sections later, we read: "By its very nature private property has a social quality which is based on the law of the common destination of earthly goods. If this social quality is overlooked, property often becomes an occasion of passionate desires for wealth and serious disturbances." Material possession ought to be a means for our turning away from ourselves to meet the needs of others. It is the influence of sin that entices us to precisely the opposite. When this happens, we turn God's blessings into a curse.

Private property comes with the moral obligation to use that property in accord with the common good. These obligations are both the source of our personal economic freedom—we must be free to fulfill our obligations—and the moral limits on what we may do with the material goods we possess. Insofar as we have an obligation to use our property in accord with the common good, the state must respect that legitimate freedom. But the state also has obligations. Among them is the duty to protect the common good, including seeing to it that the basic needs of all citizens are met. When individuals fail in their duty to use their wealth for the sake of others, it invites the intervention of the state. On the other hand, when the state unnecessarily interferes with the proper freedom of individuals to justly dispose of their private property according to their best judgment (and there are near-infinite ways to use wealth well), then the state not only violates the rights of the individual but also erodes the ability of individuals to fulfill the obligations placed on them by the material goods entrusted to their care. When civil society, including individuals, fails in regard to its obligations to the common good, it invites government intrusion. When government intrudes unnecessarily, it usurps the proper role of civil society and erodes confidence in government.

The proper use of material goods by individuals or the state has implications for what the Church calls the preferential option for the poor. It is often said that justice is blind. This is misleading. Justice treats equal things equally, which means that, all else being equal, a rich man and a poor man should receive the same treatment before the law. But justice that is blind to relevant differences is not justice. Justice treats different things differently. Justice is not blind, for example, to innocence and guilt. Neither should justice be blind to need. If one child is sick and another healthy, who gets the medicine should not be a blindly answered question.

If you can understand why the medicine would go to the sick child, you can understand the Church's preferential option for the poor. The poor are least able to care for themselves materially and should be shown special preference *as a matter of justice*. So it is a good thing that, in everything from medical care to tax policy, U.S. law gives the advantage to those who are least able to care for themselves. That's not to say that our laws get every policy question right but that the basic principle is nearly universally accepted in the United States by Republicans and Democrats alike.

If that doesn't sound quite right, consider the following: Federal, state, and local governments in the United States spend just under 40 percent of the nation's gross domestic product every year. That means for every dollar produced by the U.S. economy, somewhere between one-third and two-fifths of it gets spent by a government. Much of this is simply redistribution. In fact, in 2007, the final year before the Great Recession, the federal government spent about $1.45 trillion, almost half its total budget, on programs that essentially transfer wealth from those who have more to those who have less.[12] Keep this in mind next time you hear a conversation about whether or not the United States should redistribute wealth. We already do. Redistribution is the status quo.

Of course, there are limits on what government can do for political, and economic, and moral reasons. As Pope Francis wrote in *Laudato Si'*, "Helping the poor financially must always be a provisional solution in the face of pressing needs. The broader objective should always be to allow them a dignified life through work." The poor deserve our assistance as a matter of justice. But the poor are not a problem to be solved or a burden to be borne. They are people, with all the dignity that entails.

The poor are not a problem to be solved or a burden to be borne. They are people with all the dignity that entails.

The preferential option for the poor and the universal destination of material goods are not simply talking points for conversations about big policy questions. They affect, or ought to affect, decisions we make every day. Who among us can honestly say that they see the things God has given to them, again as it is written in *Gaudium et Spes*, as "not only as his own but also as common in the sense that they should be able to benefit not only him but also others?" And who among us can honestly say that we do enough to make care for the poor a priority in our own lives?

---

12 Jeffrey A. Miron, "Rethinking Redistribution," *National Affairs* 6 (2011).

Where we shop, what we buy, how hard we work, how well we treat our coworkers and employees, how we invest our money, how we invest our time, how well we save, how much we waste—all of these are questions of everyday significance that shape how we live our citizenship. It is tempting to think of economic choices as morally neutral, as simple calculations of cost and efficiency, but the way we use our money matters.

Materialism and consumerism are rampant in our culture. We see them everywhere, and yet, like an iceberg, so much of our culture's consumerism lies hidden. Some sins of greed are comparatively easy for most Americans to condemn—drug dealing, human trafficking, securities fraud—mostly sins of the economic margins, of the poor and the very wealthy. But it's not that easy. There are many ways that the easy comforts of a society as wealthy as ours can do us harm.

Amid all this incredible stuff, it's easy to lose sight of the things that really matter, which are mostly not things.

We have more material wealth than almost any society in history. We live longer, eat better (or at least more), and dwell more comfortably. We take clean water for granted, as we do electricity, heating, air conditioning, medicine, and instant access to an unimaginable amount of information and entertainment that we can stream (out of thin air!) to our phones, TVs, computers, tablets, and appliances. You get the idea. Amid all this incredible stuff, it's easy to lose sight of the things that really matter, which are mostly not things.

Our relationships are increasingly filtered through electronic devices. There's a cable news station/newspaper/

website/blog for every political and ideological niche. We, especially the younger generations, self-select our virtual friends so that, if we're honest, most of us are surrounded by people who think just like us! Pope Francis noticed this in *Laudato Si'*: "Today's media do enable us to communicate and to share our knowledge and affections. Yet at times they also shield us from direct contact with the pain, the fears and the joys of others and the complexity of their personal experiences." How many hours a day does the average child watch television? How many hours a day does the average millennial spend on social media? Our inability to "switch off" and "unplug" is a sign of the high priority we place on things, even good things, over people. It's not a good sign.

The Dignity of Work

One of the ways we build up society and provide for our families and communities is work. Since Pope Leo XIII launched Catholic social teaching with *Rerum Novarum* in 1891, the question of work and human labor has been a fundamental part of the Church's doctrine.

"Only man is capable of work," wrote Pope John Paul II in his 1981 encyclical On Human Work (*Laborem Exercens*), "and only man works, at the same time by work occupying his existence on earth. Thus work bears a particular mark of man and of humanity, the mark of a person operating within a community of persons. And this mark decides its interior characteristics; in a sense it constitutes its very nature." Work is tied to our very nature as persons and members of society.

Work is often seen as an inconvenience, a burden, or a punishment for original sin, that is, until one is deprived of work. It's not just the rewards of our labor—payment or wages—that makes work a human good. It's work itself. Unemployment and underemployment are especially detrimental to families. Being deprived of the opportunity to work makes it very difficult to contribute materially to the good of one's family and society. In such a situation in which one has no opportunity to contribute, social and familial bonds erode, and attachment to society and the common good is diminished. In extreme situations, the chronically unemployed are forced into the dehumanizing position of being mere receptacles of society's beneficence. If our humanity is expressed most fully in love through a giving of self, then being mired in a position of receptivity with no chance or expectation of contribution can be profoundly dehumanizing.

The question of a just wage is tied to the question of human labor for obvious reasons. Human labor is not a commodity that can be bought or sold for whatever price the market will allow. A man and/or woman with a family to support ought to be able to earn wages sufficient to provide for those to whom he and/or she is bound and obliged. It's true that not all work is equally valuable. But to be forced by the demands of the labor market to trade one's labor for a pittance, for a wage inadequate to the maintenance of decent living is unjust, even if the work is menial and the wage has been mutually agreed upon.

The Church has long insisted on the priority of labor over capital, which simply means the value of our labor is more precious—to us, to our family, and to society—than money, even when that money is (as it ought to be) honestly earned, creatively invested, and put at the service of humane industry. The reason for this is that our work is all we may have. Investment capital is, almost by definition, surplus.

Labor unions have traditionally provided protection to laborers. The Church, largely at the urging of U.S. bishops in the nineteenth century, has long insisted on the right of workers to organize. If individuals have the right to pool resources and share risk for the sake of creating wealth (as in the case of a company), then surely individuals have the right to organize in a similar way to share resources and mitigate risk in the labor market. At their best, both businesses and labor and trade unions serve the common good by promoting solidarity through the mechanism of subsidiary organizations. At their worst, both unions and businesses can become parasitic on the common good, manipulative of the political process, and corrupted by the desire to increase power and maximize profits at all costs—for shareholders on the one hand and union members on the other.

Capitalism?

Pope Francis has been especially critical of an economic system that does not keep concern for the human person at its heart. His criticisms are often taken to be an attack on economic freedom, but that's a mistake. His criticisms have more to do with insisting that economic freedom, like all human freedom, must be tethered to the truth about the human person, including the truth about how we ought to use the gifts we have been given. In this sense, one can find firm grounding in Catholic tradition in substance, if not style, for Pope Francis' economic criticisms.

In 1991, for example, Pope John Paul II asks in *Centesimus Annus* whether, given the collapse of communism in Europe, capitalism should be understood as the "path to true economic and civil progress?" "The answer," he insisted, "is obviously complex." It depends on what one means by capitalism. He continues:

If by "capitalism" is meant an economic system which recognizes the fundamental and positive role of business, the market, private property and the resulting responsibility for the means of production, as well as free human creativity in the economic sector, then the answer is certainly in the affirmative... if by "capitalism" is meant a system in which freedom in the economic sector is not circumscribed within a strong juridical framework which places it at the service of human freedom in its totality...then the reply is certainly negative.

Pope Francis has criticized "so-called unrestrained liberalism," by which I take him to mean something like Pope St. John Paul II's second definition of capitalism as an approach to economics that acknowledges no moral limits on economic freedom beyond whatever limits are imposed by the market itself. Importantly, this critique of unguided economic freedom remains in force whether the market in question is regulated by the government or not. Some things must not be done, even if the law and market allow them.

This criticism is a challenge both to those who would put too much faith in the ability of markets to produce just results (efficiency and justice are not the same thing) and those who see economic problems as a technical question, as if everything will fall into place if we could just get the regulation right.

Pope Benedict XVI, in his encyclical *Caritas in Veritate*, warned that thinking of society as a tug of war between the market and the state was dangerous, precisely because such thinking fails to account for the place where most of our lives happen, the place where solidarity finds its natural home: "The exclusively binary model of market-plus-State is corrosive of society, while economic forms based on solidarity, which find their natural home in civil society without being restricted to it, build up society."

If we wish to build up society, and that is our vocation as Catholic citizens, then we must resist the temptation to see our work as a balancing act between economic and political power. Both must be made to serve the good of society, a reality that requires good laws, responsible economics, and above all, a healthy and humane culture to guide them both.

CHAPTER

Freedom and Law

We live in a democratic republic, founded on certain principles of law and drawing on a certain understanding of the ends of political life and the best means of achieving those ends. Our political and legal arrangements have a particular history and also particular strengths and weaknesses. Democracy promotes and protects equality, but it can also diminish excellence because everyone has a say, both the wise and the foolish. Our political freedom, at least in principle, allows us to live largely as we see fit, without undue interference from government. But that also means we are free to abuse our freedom and use it toward selfish or destructive ends. Our economic prosperity represents a singular achievement, but being rich (at least as a whole, we are incredibly rich) cannot in itself make us good. We are a deeply religious nation, but we are also a nation where a maddening variety of religious ideas flourish, the good along with the wicked.

The fabric of American life, with all its variety, shapes who we are as citizens and also shapes how we exercise our citizenship.

I sometimes joke that two of the most typically American phrases one hears (and we hear them all the time) are: "It's a free country," and, "There should be a law against that!" These two sentences capture a fundamental tension in U.S. politics. When someone tries to tell us to change our behavior, we invoke freedom as a defense, and when someone else uses his or her freedom in ways we don't like, we appeal to public authority to put an end to the "misbehavior."

But if freedom is a good thing, then why do we have so many laws to limit freedom? And if laws are the only things to keep people from abusing their freedom, then how free are we? Isn't it a contradiction for Americans to proudly think we are both a free country and a nation of laws?

There are two ways to resolve this apparent contradiction. The first is simply to aim for the most agreeable balance between freedom and prohibition. There is something to be said for this approach, even if it's easier said than done. Our Constitution was designed to produce compromise or at least to prevent the majority from tyrannizing the minority. Our politics are often marked by gridlocked legislatures and politicians who seem all too willing to compromise their principles for the sake of political expedience. But these headaches are a byproduct of a system that makes it very difficult for one faction or another to impose its will on the whole country. Even in a political environment as polarized as ours is today, when each major political party complains loudly about how its opponents want to impose their rigid ideology on the nation, neither side seems capable of winning a decisive victory. The United States is not on the verge of becoming a libertarian utopia, any more than we are on the verge of becoming a socialist one. Most Americans wouldn't want to live in either.

Our political system forces compromise and disadvantages extremism. It doesn't eliminate political extremism, of course, but it does handicap it, which is why our politics can seem so contentious from day to day and election to election. It's also why political radicalism rarely succeeds in U.S. politics in the long run. Even the most successful grassroots movements have succeeded mostly at the margins and by moving toward the political center. Major restructuring of political and social arrangements has been rare in U.S. history. It has been usually only accomplished when there has been very widespread support (passage of the New Deal, for example) or things grow so dire that citizens take up arms (as in the War for Independence and the Civil War).

The recent redefinition of marriage by the Supreme Court in *Obergefell v. Hodges* is a notable exception to this rule, just as the judicial imposition of the current abortion culture was in *Roe v. Wade*. The latter case has led to more than forty years of deeply divisive politics, the central front in what have come to be known as the "culture wars." The latter may well prove to have a similar effect.

But back to our question about law and freedom. There is another way to resolve the apparent tension between law and freedom, and that's by realizing that freedom needs law and good law needs freedom. At their best, the two aren't in tension, let alone contradictory. Law makes freedom possible and freedom is the best guarantee of good laws. But this is only true if we understand freedom as something more than the right or ability to simply do as we please. Freedom is only really free when it is tied to the truth. Human law can only protect true freedom when it acknowledges its own limits, when our laws recognize that they do not create truth but instead try to recognize and embody truth without claiming to be its author.

This understanding of law has been present since the very beginning of our nation. It is why the Declaration of Independence insists that the most fundamental rights are not the creation or gift of human laws and governments but come from a higher source: "We hold these truths to be self-evident, that all men are created equal, that they are endowed by their

Creator with certain unalienable Rights." In fact, the legitimacy of government itself depends on the acknowledgment of its own limits. The law to which the Declaration appeals to justify its claims to independence is not a human law at all but "the Laws of Nature and of Nature's God."

No human law, not even the Constitution, can claim legitimacy apart from the limits imposed on it by a higher law. As Jesus said, "Repay to Caesar what belongs to Caesar and to God what belongs to God" (Mark 12:17). Human law has its necessary and proper place, and we could not "repay to Caesar what belongs to Caesar" if it did not. But Caesar is not God, and when Caesar fails to acknowledge his own limits, bad things happen.

So law must acknowledge the truth of its own limits, but what about my claim that freedom requires law? To show what I mean, consider what it requires to play an instrument. Any child can bang on a keyboard, making all kinds of noise. (Speaking from experience as a former child and current father, kids actually enjoy this, even if it's a headache for everyone else.) There is a sort of freedom in this noisemaking. It requires no practice, there are no rules to follow, and the child just clangs merrily away. But it's only a sort of freedom, because the one thing the ham-fisted kid at the keyboard isn't "free" to do is actually *play* the piano.

A kid banging on a keyboard is not playing the piano. Not really. He's certainly not making music. *Really* playing the piano, really making music, is something that has to be learned through study and practice. A musician has to know which keys play which notes, where they are, and their relation to one another. He or she must know which notes are in which scales, about harmonies, when and how to play soft or loud, and a thousand other things. But even knowing all these things isn't enough. If a musician wants to play beautiful music, he or she is going to have to practice and needs the discipline to keep practicing even when not feeling like it. Our budding pianist is also going to need, most likely, a good teacher, someone to teach the rules and correct the mistakes.

Only then is our pianist really free to play the piano and to create new and beautiful music. All that practice and discipline didn't make our pianist less free but more free. The same applies to politics and citizenship. If we want to be free, we need to follow the rules that keep our society free.

If human law defines right and wrong, if "justice" is whatever the law says it is, then there can be no freedom. To say that justice is whatever the law says it is, in fact, is akin to saying that any combination of notes pounded out on a piano is as good as any other combination of notes. There's no difference between Mozart and "Billy," the ham-fisted boy. It's all subjective. And the disciplined freedom that makes great music and good laws becomes meaningless.

But of course, right and wrong are not determined by the whim or will of the majority. Awful turns of the twentieth century, from the Nazi Holocaust to the Soviet Gulags, should have taught us that. In our own nation, slavery was not only legal for a long time but also protected by the Constitution. Did that make it right? Did that make it just? Of course not.

Law defends and protects justice. Law seeks to bring about justice. But law does not and cannot make something right or wrong, just or unjust. Why do we have laws at all? And if our laws cannot tell us what is good and just, then what can? If law is not the source of justice, what is?

If self-government is to be good government, then it makes sense that the "selves" doing the governing would have to be good. The citizens of a nation like ours, if they were to remain free, would have to be the kind of people capable of living freedom well. Likewise, if we want to be governed by good and just laws, then we'll have to expect our lawmakers to be the kinds of people who understand justice and real freedom. No one wants a tin-eared piano teacher who can't play. No one wants to inherit the flaws of his or her teacher. Pupils of such a teacher won't make good piano players.

In a republic like ours, we elect those who represent us. We entrust to them the duty of writing our laws and governing our nation, but we do not delegate our citizenship to them. Electing good representatives to government is not the goal of good citizenship. In fact, good government is not the goal of good citizenship. This gets things exactly backward. The goal of good government is to allow members of the community to live well, which means to live freedom in accord with the truth.

We need virtuoso citizens. In Christian terms, we need disciples. More than that, we need citizen saints.

Just as a bad piano teacher will not produce proficient pupils, bad students will never make good pianists no matter how masterful the teacher. A student's task is not to make his teacher look good; it's to learn to play well. In the United States today, we often blame our social ills on our laws and our politicians. Although they are far from being blameless, we must not shy away from taking a hard look at ourselves to understand the real challenges facing our nation. We need virtuoso citizens. In Christian terms, we need disciples. More than that, we need citizen saints.

That's not something even the best government with the best laws can accomplish on its own. If we live only as well as the laws require us to live, then we're in trouble. If we confuse what is legal with what is right, we expect more of the law than the law can provide. Put another way, good laws still require good, public-minded citizens who will respect the law and follow it, rather than small-minded, self-interested citizens who will abuse the law and twist it to their advantage.

The work of Catholic citizenship, like the work of Christian discipleship itself, is a vocation, a response to a call. Like all vocations, the idea of the thing pales in comparison to the lived reality and experience. Citizenship is the same way. Citizenship requires a commitment to the right principles, but it also demands wisdom, patience, perseverance, discernment, and prudence. And like any other vocation, the vocation to citizenship begins with love.

CHAPTER

Growing in Faith and Growing in Virtue

Chances are, if you're reading this book, it's because you already understand that the way we live our Catholic faith shapes, and ought to shape, the society in which we live. So far, we've looked at the ideas that undergird the Catholic vision of society. We've discussed the importance of human dignity and the sanctity of human life as the foundation for all of the Church's social teaching. We've underscored the importance of civil society. We've considered the importance of government but have also shown how our rights and responsibilities are exercised and met mostly in that space between our individual selves and the state, the laws of which guide and govern our nation. And we've seen how being a good citizen means growing in virtue so that we are better able to live our freedom well and to show others how to do the same.

Citizenship, after all, is about membership in a community. At each layer of our social life, we find communities that rely on and bolster other communities. When one part is weak, the other parts suffer. When one part is strong, it reinforces the others. Solidarity makes subsidiarity possible, and subsidiarity is a catalyst for solidarity. Both serve the common good, which is the best guarantee of the good of individuals.

In this chapter, we'll turn to some practical steps we can take, here and now, to better live out our vocation as Catholic citizens. Specifically, we'll look at four arenas in which our faith can be brought to bear on those parts of our common life we've already discussed: in our families, in the Church, in our communities, and in our nation. Each section of this chapter will include seven suggestions (seven being a nice biblical number) for concrete steps we can all take to strengthen our families, build up the Church, and restore the communities and nation in which we live and to which we belong.

Strengthening Our Families

Say "Please," "Thank you," "I'm sorry." Beginning in late 2014, Pope Francis began devoting his Wednesday audiences to a catechesis on the family. One of the more memorable reflections was on the importance of using these three phrases in family life. Here's part of what the pontiff said:

> These expressions open up the way to living well in your family, to living in peace. They are simple expressions, but not so simple to put into practice! They hold much power: the power to keep home life intact even when tested with a thousand problems. But if they are absent, little holes can start to crack open and the whole thing may even collapse.

> These simple words are like the oil in a car's engine, unglamorous, but without them there is friction, which causes heat, wear and tear, and eventually, catastrophic problems.

Eat meals as a family. Today's world makes family dinners difficult, especially when both spouses work. But the time spent together around the table—free from the distractions of work, homework, television, smartphones, video games, and all the other noise we let into our lives—is one of the best ways to facilitate communication within the family. Most of us know from experience that it is all too easy to live under the same roof as someone and go through days without slowing down and having an actual conversation with them. The dinner hour is a perfect time and place to slow down, unplug, and reconnect with those closest to us. Experts always say that one of the biggest sources of friction within marriage and the family is lack of communication. It's hard to communicate if there's never time. Make family dinner that time.

And Mom and Dad, make time for a date night. Schedule it. We live in a culture that often puts too high a premium on romance and feelings and not enough emphasis on sacrifice and the hard work of loving people who are sinners just like us. But that's not a problem we're going to solve by depriving our own marriages of romance. Our lives are busy. Take time to spend "alone time" with the one you have chosen to face life's ups and downs. Your marriage will be stronger for it, and strong marriages make for strong families.

Family prayer. I have kids. I know a family rosary is asking a lot of a three year old. I know kids at Mass can be a hassle. But if I can't make the effort to get my family to Mass once a week, what does that say about my priorities? What does it teach my kids about what's really important? If my kids don't see my wife and me at prayer, how will they learn to do the same? And Mass isn't about fulfilling an obligation (although Catholics are obliged). It is about giving thanks for all we have (including, yes, our family). It really is true that going to Mass and sharing in the sacrifice of the altar is the most important thing any of us does. Prayer, especially the Mass, changes us. It shapes us and helps make us more like our Father in heaven. Making Mass a fixture of family life shows that God is a priority and reminds everyone that the family itself is a participation in sacred things.

Moreover, for husbands and wives, the Mass ought to be a reminder of just what they aspire to in their marriage. The relationship between husband and wife is a sign (literally, a *sacrament*) of the love between Christ and his Church. Want to see marriage vows lived perfectly? Pay attention to how Christ loves his Church in the Eucharist. Want to learn how to love better? Spend time with Love himself.

Family service. Family is where we learn, first and most profoundly, our responsibility for others. Learning to love is challenge enough within a family. Learning to love those outside the family, even complete strangers, helps to put Christian love into a different context. Visit a retirement home, collect canned goods at Thanksgiving, or lend a hand at the local soup kitchen. All these things are a reminder that love isn't just about getting along with the people you live with for the sake of convenience: "This is how all will know that you are my disciples, if you have love for one another" (John 13:35). Acts of service reinforce a sense of common purpose and shared responsibility and provide a powerful example for kids of all ages (even teenagers!). Crucially, service work is a powerful antidote to the faith becoming merely about ideas or rules of behavior. Christianity is about the encounter of the risen Christ and sharing the love of him who first loved us. As St. James reminds us, faith without works is dead (James 2:17).

Reach out to other families. It's not always easy to live out family life in an intentionally Catholic way. Finding other families who have the same priorities can be reassuring to parents, who can sometimes feel beset by a culture with very different priorities. It's also important for kids to know that their family isn't the only one living a little bit differently. At the same time, strong families can be a beacon of light and hope in a world where they are all too rare. Strong families are attractive. Don't be afraid to let others see your family living their faith! And don't be afraid that others might see your family's imperfections. Nobody's family is perfect, but we should be confident that we can be an example for other families by striving for something good. As is always the case with discipleship, it's not about pointing to ourselves but about living in a way that points to Christ. Don't underestimate the power of the family to evangelize, especially in a culture so filled with broken and damaged families.

Defend marriage and human life. There are countless ways we can help build a culture of life in and through our families, beginning with being open to life ourselves. Pray outside an abortion clinic for the unborn, their mothers and fathers, and for abortionists. Join a parish or diocesan group that travels to the annual March for Life in Washington, D.C. Support, with your time and money, your parish or diocesan pro-life ministries. Support local crisis-pregnancy centers. Compassion and assistance for women in difficult pregnancies or women who have had abortions are other ways you can help. It can be difficult to speak about the defense of life even within our own families. Taking a public stand on such a divisive, politically charged issue can be still more difficult. But we must not remain silent. Building a culture of life requires us to defend life in the womb, and increasingly, those at the end of their lives. Failure to defend life at its beginning and end makes a mockery of our claims to care for the lives of the poor, the immigrant, the handicapped, and all the rest on the peripheries of society.

It can seem at times as if current history has left the Church's understanding of marriage in the past. As Catholics, we must not be discouraged by failure, either ours or those of our loved ones. We need to be living reminders that happy families and strong marriages are not an impossible ideal. As Pope Francis has said:

> The most persuasive testimony of the blessing of Christian marriage is the good life of Christian spouses and of the family. There is no better way to speak of the beauty of the sacrament! A marriage consecrated by God safeguards that bond between man and woman that God has blessed from the very creation of the world; and it is the source of peace and goodness for the entire lifetime of the marriage and family.

We must also be willing to speak the truth about marriage with love and compassion. Defending the truth about marriage these days can be exceedingly difficult. It may well be that the Church, as a whole and in its members, will suffer greatly by defending marriage. But proclaiming the Gospel has always required courage, no less today than ever before. The Church's teaching on marriage and God's plan for human sexuality are precious gifts and part of the Good News. Nothing is gained by hiding them under a bushel basket. Above all, we must let love, true love, be our strongest argument.

Catholic education begins at home. Parents are the primary teachers of their children. This is more than just a nice thought. It's a fact of family life. Our kids pick up our virtues and vices. They learn, whether we mean to teach them or not. So in addition to setting a good example by our behavior, it's important that parents take seriously our obligation to teach our children about the faith. This means, among other things, that Catholic parents need to be well-informed about their faith so that they can pass it on to their children. How often do we read Scripture? (Saint Jerome said, "Ignorance of Scripture is ignorance of Christ.") Do we own a *Catechism*? Do we ever open it? Read the *Lives of the Saints* with your kids, or watch the "Catholicism" DVD series by Fr. (now Bishop) Robert Barron as a family. There is so much to learn about our faith and the amazing men and women who have lived it over the millennia. Our faith isn't a relic to be handed down. It's an adventure to be lived!

Building Up the Church

Much of what we have said about strengthening the family touches directly or indirectly on the way our participation in the life of the Church also shapes the society in which we live. So, now we turn to ways that we can build up the most important community to which we belong, the body of Christ, the Church.

Care for your conscience. We are each bound to follow our conscience, but we are also responsible for striving to make sure our conscience is well-formed. This means taking the time to listen to the wisdom of the Church about the choices we face and having the humility to know the limits of our own wisdom. Having a conscience doesn't free us to make whatever choice we want. Conscience is not an expression of our own willfulness. Rather, conscience is how we discover, as the Second Vatican Council's Declaration on Religious Freedom (*Dignitatis Humanae*) puts it, "a law which he has not laid upon himself but which he must obey." Given that our own sin can cloud and distort our conscience, it is important to cultivate good habits (virtues) and to seek forgiveness when we sin. This bring us to our next point.

Go to confession; go to Mass. If "please," "thank you," and "I'm sorry" are important in the family, these words are essential in the Church as well. Eucharist means "thanksgiving," and in the Mass, we give thanks to the Father for the gift of his son, Jesus Christ. Every worthy reception of Communion joins us in a profound way to Christ himself and to every member of his body, living and dead. In the sacrament of penance, we ask and receive pardon for our sins, for those things by which we have separated ourselves from God and from one another. In the sacrament, we are reconciled not only with God but also with the entire body of Christ, the Church. Reconciliation and Communion are powerful antidotes to the division and individualism of our broken world.

Support your parish financially. Tithe, if you can. If you can't give 10 percent, give what you can. Give until it hurts. We've already discussed the immense contributions the Church makes to civil society through its charitable works. Most of us can't spend all of our time running a hospital or an inner-city school or an adoption agency, but we can support our brothers and sisters in Christ who do. Give generously and know that God will not be outdone in generosity. As an added bonus, generosity helps detach us from material things. Remember the story of the rich young man from the Gospel!

Give your time. A more precious commodity is hard to find. Often, it is easier to write a check than to set aside time in our busy lives to help others. There's nothing wrong, nothing at all, with giving financially, but the work of discipleship has to involve our whole lives, not just our wallets. When we give our time, when we show up in person to work with others face to face, we're not just giving something we *have* but something of *who we are*. Be warned: This is how relationships and friendships are formed. Don't be surprised if sharing your time leads to bonding with new and wonderful people!

Every parish in the country has social-outreach ministries. I've never known a parish where there simply was not enough need to meet the generosity of the parishioners. Volunteer for bingo night or to work in the parish food pantry. Join a Catholic organization like the Knights of Columbus or the Legion of Mary. Ask your pastor what ministries need more volunteers. If your parish doesn't have a ministry suited to your schedule or talents, look to the diocese or a neighboring parish, or talk to your pastor about starting a new ministry in your own parish.

Support Catholic schools. Not everyone can attend a Catholic school, but there are millions of children, including many non-Catholics, who do. Schools that form souls while they educate young minds are an invaluable resource to the Church and to society as a whole. Catholic education is something the Church in the United States has done very well historically, but Catholic school systems across the country face tremendous challenges today.

Invite people to the Church. Maybe you have a neighbor who was raised Catholic but has stopped practicing. Maybe you have a neighbor who isn't Catholic but is curious to find out more about the Church. You might be surprised to find out how many people will take the first step toward, or the first step back toward, the Church if they are simply offered an invitation. But be prepared to invest time in newcomers you bring to your parish. The parish ought to be a community bound together in faith, yes, but also by personal relationships and, hopefully, friendships. What kind of a host invites a guest and then has no time for the guest once she arrives? These things take time. And by that, I mean your time and my time. Can we make time for building up the Church by bringing others into it? If not, why not?

Defend religious freedom. What can each of us do to defend religious freedom? First, we can live lives worthy of that freedom. The right to religious freedom arises because we have a duty to serve God and others. The right to serve God as we ought does not cease when we fail in that duty, but it does undermine the credibility of our witness as Catholics when we demand our right to live as Catholics and then abuse and squander that right by living however we please. Dedicating ourselves to religious freedom doesn't mean segregating our faith from public life. In fact, it means just the opposite. It is to insist that religion plays a crucial and irreplaceable role in shaping good citizens and sustaining the common good. The value of religion is hardly limited to its social utility, but we must never tire of showing by the way we live our lives the truth that religion is an indispensable public good.

Restoring Our Communities and Our Nation

If we want our politics to serve the common good, then we need a solid foundation. As we've seen, strong families and a vibrant Church are crucial to the health of civil society. We can't have a healthy nation unless these foundational institutions are in good order. Of course, as the principle of subsidiarity reminds us, the flourishing of civil society is both a cause of healthy politics and the result of healthy politics.

Meet your neighbors. This is elementary, but these days it bears repeating. Do you know your neighbors by name? Introduce yourself. Got a front porch? Try sitting on it and saying hello to people who walk past. Shovel the sidewalk for the elderly couple down the block, or bring some brownies to the new family that just moved in. Organize a block party. Being sociable with your neighbors isn't just about old-fashioned politeness, either. You don't have to be the neighborhood busybody, but anonymity undermines a shared sense of responsibility for one another and for the places we share as a common home. You can't depend on your neighbors, and they can't depend on you, if you don't know each other.

Celebrate the Fourth of July. And Memorial Day, Labor Day, Veterans Day, and all the rest of the civic holidays we so easily (and mistakenly) take for granted. Read the Declaration of Independence and the Constitution at least once a year. Enjoy the fireworks. Fly the flag. Be proud to be an American. Cynicism about our public institutions is deeply corrosive to the kind of affection and attachment to our nation that is the foundation for good citizenship. We cannot truly serve the good of our nation if we do not love it, and it is very hard to love something for which you feel nothing. Public holidays are to citizenship what a good date night is to a marriage. These holidays remind us that, despite all our flaws, this nation to which we belong is capable of aspiring to, and at times attaining, great things. Our country is worth the effort. It's certainly worth a celebration now and then.

Work for disagreement. That's not a typo. American society is marked by all kinds of divisions, especially when it comes to politics. It is often easier to assume that someone with whom we disagree is acting out of bad faith or simple ignorance. Real disagreement is achieved when we realize that stupidity and ill will are not the only explanations, indeed, not even the most likely explanations for differences of opinion about important matters in public life. Disagreement, at least the kind of disagreement I'm talking about, is a mark of civility and an achievement necessary for the proper functioning of a political body as diverse as ours. Real disagreement is achieved only when we strive to understand the best reasons for why someone else might think or act differently than we do. By striving to understand our opponent's point of view, as our opponent understands it, we can address our differences without imputing motives. More importantly, by identifying what it is we actually disagree about, we can move beyond name calling and speculation about motives and begin the hard work of forging compromise.

Take pride in your work and share the fruits of your labors. Most of us spend most of our lives working to make a living. We labor in this life because of the Fall (Genesis 3), but our work is also an opportunity to share in God's plan of creation. When we see work in this light, both our own work and the work of others, we better grasp the dignity of work and understand why one's labor is not just another commodity. Work is a blessing, a sacred duty, and because of this, a right. This is a crucial lesson for both employers and employees.

The ranks of great saints are filled with men and women who exhort us to love in small and ordinary ways. Our work, however exciting or menial, is no exception. As for what we do with the fruits of our labors, that is another challenge in itself. Pope Leo XIII beautifully summed up the proper Christian attitude toward material possessions when he wrote in *Rerum Novarum*:

> God has not created us for the perishable and transitory things of earth, but for things heavenly and everlasting; He has given us this world as a place of exile, and not as our abiding place. As for riches and the other things which men call good and desirable, whether we have them in abundance, or are lacking in them–so far as eternal happiness is concerned–it makes no difference; the only important thing is to use them aright.

Everything we have is a gift, given to us for the sake of serving God and others. Our economic choices have moral implications. We must be good stewards of these gifts and always be ready to give back what is only ours for the time being. Our true reward is elsewhere.

Stay well-informed. The emphasis here is on "well." This is both easier and, in some ways, more difficult in an age of information overload. With so much bias in the media, and the bias cuts both ways, it is helpful to get information from numerous sources. As tricky as media bias can be, there's also a danger in listening only to voices with whom you already agree. (I find news aggregators online to be very helpful. RealClearPolitics.com offers a balance of competing views on any number of topics. For Catholic news and commentary, NewAdvent.org is an excellent place to start.) Find a Catholic website or subscribe to a Catholic newspaper, journal, or magazine. Read good books from reliable publishers (like this one!). The USCCB website (usccb.org) has some tremendous resources and information on all kinds of topics, from family and marriage, to the protection of life, to Catholic charities, to care for immigrants, to religious freedom. I'd be remiss if I didn't mention the bishops' document on Catholic citizenship, "Forming Consciences for Faithful Citizenship." It is not a long document, it's free, and it's worth your time. Its extensive treatment of conscience is especially noteworthy.

Know the men and women who represent you. Not just your representative in Congress or your senator. Know your state representatives and senators, your mayor and city council member, and your school board members. We elect public officials to represent us, not to rule over us. If you want your representatives to actually represent you, then it makes sense to keep tabs on what they do and say. What are their priorities?

Are they people of character? Don't be shy about calling their offices or writing letters to let them know what you think. Sometimes, we treat our elected leaders as some sort of modern-day aristocracy. Nonsense. We honor and respect elected offices, not because of the men and women who hold those offices, but because they serve us.

Vote. Finally, we have arrived at the ballot box! By the time you or I walk into a voting booth, most of our work of citizenship needs to have been done. And chances are, the way you vote is going to reflect the way you live your life as a citizen. If we as Catholics do not let our faith shape the way we live our lives and the way we vote, then we are failing our nation and our fellow citizens by withholding from them what we know to be best in our own lives.

Pope Benedict XVI, in *Deus Caritas Est*, wrote of the Church's role in shaping politics: "The Church cannot and must not take upon herself the political battle to bring about the most just society possible. She cannot and must not replace the State. Yet at the same time she cannot and must not remain on the sidelines in the fight for justice." We, as Catholic citizens, cannot remain on the sidelines.

When Catholics enter the voting booth with well-formed consciences and use their ballot not simply to exercise a right but as the fulfillment of a citizen's duty to defend human dignity and strive for the common good, our nation will be better for it. But voting is never enough. As we've seen over and over again, good citizenship requires a conscious effort to build our communities, serve our neighbors, strengthen our families, bring dignity to our workplace, and use material gifts well. In short, it requires living a life that shows the full dignity of the human vocation in service of the common good. As Catholics, we are uniquely positioned to show what good citizenship looks like. Now we must do it.

CONCLUSION

CALLED TO BE CITIZENS; CALLED TO BE SAINTS

Our nation was founded to be a refuge of freedom, a great experiment to see if self-limiting government in the service of liberty for the sake of the common good was possible. It was from the first, and will always remain, an experiment. The success of that project is not now, nor ever has been, guaranteed to succeed.

Our Founding Fathers knew this. In the first of the Federalist Papers, Alexander Hamilton wrote that the (as yet unratified) Constitution represented a monumental test of "whether societies of men are really capable or not of establishing good government from reflection and choice, or whether they are forever destined to depend for their political constitutions on accident and force." In his Gettysburg address, Abraham Lincoln addressed this same question by asking whether this or any nation, "conceived in liberty and dedicated to the proposition that all men are created equal can long endure," and ends on a note of hope that "government of the people, by the people, for the people, shall not perish from the earth." The survival of our nation and the success of the American project has never been a given, not in 1787, not in 1863, not today.

This truth, that freedom must never be taken for granted, is also found in Catholic social teaching. When he visited the United States in 2008, Pope Benedict XVI noted that freedom entails responsibility and requires sacrifice. Without these, freedom cannot last:

> Freedom is not only a gift, but also a summons to personal responsibility. Americans know this from experience—almost every town in this country has its monuments honoring those who sacrificed their lives in defense of freedom, both at home and abroad. The preservation of freedom calls for the cultivation of virtue, self-discipline, sacrifice for the common good and a sense of responsibility towards the less fortunate. It also demands the courage to engage in civic life and to bring one's deepest beliefs and values to reasoned public debate. In a word, freedom is ever new. It is a challenge held out to each generation, and it must constantly be won over for the cause of good.[13]

This should be a sobering reminder to us of the importance of our task as citizens. "As Christians we firmly believe," wrote Pope John Paul II in 1991, "that if there is no ultimate truth to guide and direct political activity, then ideas and convictions can easily be manipulated for reasons of power. As history demonstrates, a democracy without values easily turns into open or thinly disguised totalitarianism" (*Centesimus Annus*). Our primary task as Catholic citizens is to ensure that the values of our nation accord with the truth about the human person, the truth about human society, and the common good. If we fail in this task—and all that is required for failure is that we remain silent and do nothing—then who or what will guide our nation toward the truth that makes freedom worth living?

---

13 Address of His Holiness Benedict XVI. The White House, Washington, D.C. April 16, 2008.

The vocation of all Catholic citizens is to enter into this task for the good of our families, our Church, our neighbors, and the nation. We cannot, as citizens and Catholics, sit idly by. It is our sacred duty to educate ourselves and form our consciences (always with the Church!) so that in things large and small, we might judge rightly—at the ballot box, yes, but more importantly, in our daily lives—in those innumerable choices that make up the lion's share of our contribution to a free and just society. An article from June 12, 2012 in CatholicVote.org states there is nothing we can do to better serve and defend our democracy than to live every single day as good and faithful Catholics.

A democracy without values easily turns into open or thinly disguised totalitarianism.

The paths we must walk toward our common goal are different for each of us, but it is helpful to consider some ways each of us can work to make ourselves better citizens, and that begins with working to make ourselves better disciples. That is the great task of a citizen: to work to make our nation good. The difference that our Catholic faith makes has everything to do with what we mean by "good."

As Catholics, we know that how we treat our neighbor matters not only for today or tomorrow but also for eternity. We know that the material goods we are given are not just for our own enjoyment but also are part of our vocation to care for those the Lord has entrusted to us. We know by faith that our responsibilities are first to our family and those nearest to us. We also know that our responsibility does not end with the family, tribe, Church, or nation but extends to all human beings created in the image and likeness of the one who has saved us. We know that the ultimate good of political life is in service to a good far exceeding politics, that the kingdoms of this world will not last, and that the kingdom of God will never end.

The best thing we could ever do for ourselves, our families, our Church, our communities, and our nation is to live a life of holiness. And as the Second Vatican Council reminds us in the Dogmatic Constitution on the Church (*Lumen Gentium*), we are all called to holiness:

> Thus it is evident to everyone, that all the faithful of Christ of whatever rank or status, are called to the fullness of the Christian life and to the perfection of charity; by this holiness as such a more human manner of living is promoted in this earthly society. In order that the faithful may reach this perfection, they must use their strength accordingly as they have received it, as a gift from Christ.

What does the Catholic faith have to teach us about good citizenship? By teaching that our very lives are an unmerited gift, by teaching us to pour out our lives for others, just as Christ did for us, by teaching us to be holy as our Father in heaven is holy—and providing the grace that makes this possible—our Catholic faith transforms the work of citizenship into a means for flooding the world with the Good News of the Gospel and the hope that comes with knowing the saving love of God. If you want to be a good citizen, do everything you can to become a saint!

"Be a saint!" That certainly falls into the category of things that are, shall we say, easier said than done. And if you're like me, a moment's reflection on our own sinfulness and weakness would seem to snuff out hope for such lofty goals. But we must not sell ourselves short. More to the point, we must never sell God short! With him, all things are possible, even making a saint out of a sinner like me.

As Pope St. John Paul II reminded us, we must never be afraid of the greatness to which we are called and for which we were created and redeemed:

> Do not be satisfied with mediocrity. The kingdom of heaven is for those who are determined to enter it.... Do not be afraid to be holy! Have the courage and humility to present yourselves to the world determined to be holy, since full, true freedom is born from holiness.[14]

If we take these words to heart, if we let these words transform our lives as Catholics and as citizens, then whatever else may come, we can be assured of the freedom that comes only from living in the truth.

---

14 Pope John Paul II. Message of the Holy Father to Youth Meeting in Santiago de Compostela. August 8, 1999.